C000196564

100 WALKS IN LANCASHIRE

BOB CLARE

THE CROWOOD PRESS

First published in 2015 by
The Crowood Press Ltd
Ramsbury, Marlborough
Wiltshire SN8 2HR

www.crowood.com

British Library Cataloguing-in-Publication Data
A catalogue record for this book is available from the British Library.

ISBN 978 1 84797 899 8

Mapping in this book is sourced from the following products: OS Explorer 285, 286, 287,
296, OL2, OL7, OL21 and OL41
© Crown copyright 2015 Ordnance Survey. Licence number 100038003

Every effort has been made to ensure the accuracy of this book. However, changes can
occur during the lifetime of an edition. The Publishers cannot be held responsible for any
errors or omissions or for the consequences of any reliance on the information given in
this book, but should be very grateful if walkers could let us know of any inaccuracies by
writing to us at the address above or via the website.

As with any outdoor activity, accidents and injury can occur. We strongly advise readers to
check the local weather forecast before setting out and to take an OS map. The Publishers
accept no responsibility for any injuries which may occur in relation to following the walk
descriptions contained within this book.

Graphic design and layout by Peggy Issenman, www.peggyandco.ca
Printed and bound in India by Replika Press Pvt Ltd

Contents

How to Use this Book

The walks in the book are ordered by distance, starting with the shortest at 1.6 miles and ending with the longest at 12 miles. An information panel for each walk shows the distance, start point (see below), a summary of route terrain and level of difficulty (Easy/Moderate/Difficult), OS map(s) required, and suggested pubs/cafés at the start/end of walk or *en route*.

Readers should be aware that starting point postcodes have been supplied for satnav purposes and are not indicative of exact locations. Some start points are so remote that there is no postcode.

MAPS

There are 92 maps covering the 100 walks. Some of the walks are extensions of existing routes and the information panel for these walks will tell you the distance of the short and long versions of the walk. For those not wishing to undertake the longer versions of these walks, the 'short-cuts' are shown on the map in red.

The routes marked on the maps are punctuated by a series of numbered waypoints. These relate to the same numbers shown in the walk description.

Start Points

The start of each walk is given as a postcode and also a six-figure grid reference number prefixed by two letters (which indicates the relevant square on the National Grid). More information on grid references is found on Ordnance Survey maps.

Parking

Many of the car parks suggested are public, but for some walks you will have to park on the roadside or in a lay-by. Please be considerate when leaving your car and do not block access roads or gates. Also, if parking in a pub car park for the duration of the walk, please try to avoid busy times.

COUNTRYSIDE CODE
- Consider the local community and other people enjoying the outdoors
- Leave gates and property as you find them and follow paths
- Leave no trace of your visit and take litter home
- Keep dogs under effective control
- Plan ahead and be prepared
- Follow advice and local signs

Walks Locator

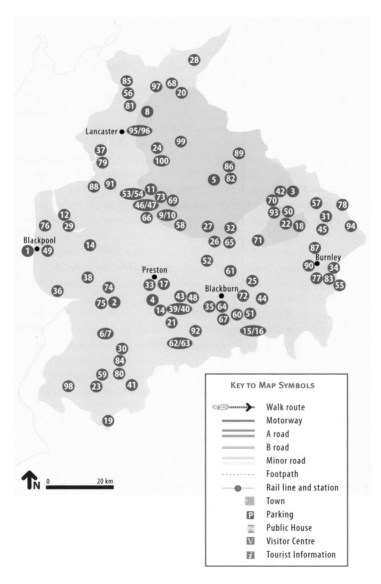

KEY TO MAP SYMBOLS

- Walk route
- Motorway
- A road
- B road
- Minor road
- Footpath
- Rail line and station
- Town
- **P** Parking
- **PH** Public House
- **V** Visitor Centre
- **i** Tourist Information

Blackpool's Golden Mile

START South Pier, Blackpool,
FY1 5AA, SD304377

FINISH North Pier

DISTANCE 1½miles (2.4km)

SUMMARY An easy stroll
along the promenade

MAP Unnecessary, but, if you
insist on checking, the route OS
Explorer 286 Blackpool & Preston

In the not too distant past Blackpool's Golden Mile could claim to be the most walked stretch of road not just in Lancashire but in the country. Of course it's not that golden – an array of amusement arcades, souvenir stalls, restaurants, hotels and attractions dominated by the looming presence of Blackpool Tower. And of course it's not a mile – it stretches between South Pier and North Pier, a distance of 1.6 miles. But it is in Lancashire and it is a good place to start.

① With the Irish Sea on your left, walk along the promenade, passing Central Pier after a mile (a real one!) and continuing until you arrive at North Pier. That's it.

② There is one more thing you might consider – a ride to the top of Blackpool Tower. Best pick a clear day for this experience. At first your eyes may be drawn seawards to the gas fields, the offshore wind turbines of Morecambe Bay and the big hump to the north-west that is Black Combe on the edge of the Lake District.

③ But turn the other way and there spread out before you is the canvas of this guide. To the north Warton Crag, and then after sweeping down to the Lune Valley comes the upland mass of the Bowland Fells. Pass over the Ribble Valley to the West Pennine Moors. A good number of walks described in the following pages are in this panorama. Over the hills there is a Lancashire beyond: Blackburn and Burnley, Pendle, Haslingden, Pendle and Rossendale. These too are represented here.

(4) Afterwards, return to the ground and the Ballroom and the Promenade, buy your kiss-me-quick hat, and enjoy a fish and chip supper on the way back to South Pier, not forgetting your little stick of Blackpool Rock. And then put on your walking boots; it is time to go and explore Lancashire.

Longton Brickcroft

START Longton Brickcroft
visitors' centre and car park,
PR4 5YY, SD479250

DISTANCE 1 mile (1.6km)

SUMMARY An easy stroll
on well-made paths

WHERE TO EAT AND DRINK
There are no facilities on site but
there are a number of pubs and
tea shops in Longton village

USEFUL WEBSITES
www.southribble.gov.uk;
www.ribblecoastandwetlands.com;
www.lancswt.org.uk
(Lancashire Wildlife Trust)

A figure-of-eight exploration of a local nature reserve on the site of a former brickworks.

1   Starting at the visitors' centre, cross the car park to its far side, entering the south pond area with water on your right. At a brisk pace it will take about 15mins to complete a circuit, though a brisk pace misses the point. The ponds are a magnet for all kinds of waterfowl so take time to stop and stare. The path follows an undulating course, which at its highest point provides a pleasing view over the pond.

2   Back at the visitors' centre cross the car park once again but, instead of turning right into the reserve, exit onto Drumacre Lane. Turn right and after 50yds turn left onto a wooded track. After passing a small pond on the left (obscured by foliage in the summer months), the way opens out at the north pond. Keep on the track, with water on the right. At the far end the track arrives at the edge of a housing estate. Keep ahead to reach Briar Grove. Turn left and left again on School Lane. Cross the road and turn right into a wedge of parkland called the Grove. Cross this to Liverpool Rd. Turn left for the Brickcroft.

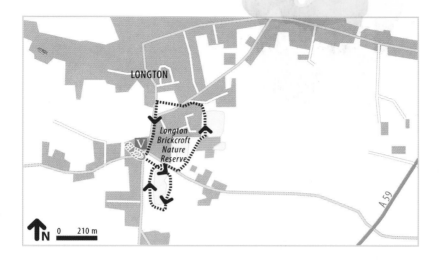

Points of interest

Longton Brickcroft is one of a number of sites around the county where industry has been supplanted by nature. Until the early 1970s clay was extracted from the area on the edge of the village of Longton. When the site was worked out it was left and within a relatively short time was colonized by plants, insects and birds. Pits became ponds – ponds that could be stocked with fish. In 1998 the Brickcroft was made into a local nature reserve managed by South Ribble Borough Council. It is recognized as an important wetland site, particularly valued for its swamp habitats. To check for the opening times of the visitors' centre, contact 01772-611497.

The Gisburn Forest Tramper Trail

START School Lane car park, Gisburn Forest, BB7 4TS, SD732562

DISTANCE 1½ miles (2.4km)

SUMMARY Tramper Category 1

MAP OS Explorer OL41 Forest of Bowland

WHERE TO EAT AND DRINK Forest Den Café at the Hub, Stephen Park

In recent years Lancashire County Council, working in partnership with the countryside services of its boroughs – the Forest of Bowland, United Utilities, the Forestry Commission and others – has opened up a number of 'Tramper' trails over the county. A tramper is a robust, motorized buggy especially designed to travel on off-road tracks. Across the county, but particularly in the Forest of Bowland, there are a number of sites where trampers can be hired (often at a nominal fee), allowing those that use them access to Lancashire's wonderful countryside.

① Facing Stocks Reservoir, take the footpath in the right corner, which is the start of the circular walk. This passes first the picnic area and then a tramper-friendly track to a birdwatching hide.

② Almost 800yds from the start at a marker post turn right onto a much narrower track entering woods. In a little over 200yds this arrives at a junction in more open ground. Turn right. Now on a broader track keep ahead through tall trees.

③ Keep on the track as it swings right, crossing a culvert, and descends through broadleaf woodland to bring you back on the footpath close to the car park. Turn left.

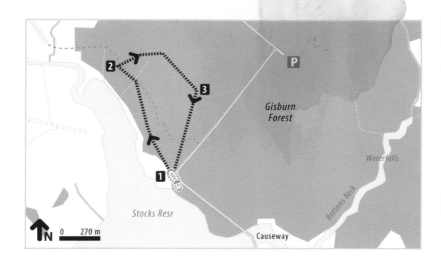

Points of interest

The location at the start of the walk lies close to Lancashire's lost village of Stocks. Indeed, the ruins of the old church can be seen to the rear of the car park. In the 1920s, as Blackpool was becoming more and more popular and attracting millions of visitors, it faced a problem with water supply. To resolve this situation the Fylde Waterboard constructed a dam and flooded the head of the Hodder Valley to create the reservoir. The project required an army of over 500 men at its height. Although outside the area of flooding, the church, vicarage, school and a number of farms were demolished to protect water quality. Now this whole area – forest and reservoir – is an outdoor playground cared for by United Utilities and the Forestry Commission. Apart from the place's obvious attraction to walkers, there is a fishery on the reservoir and the Forest of Gisburn is a magnet to mountain bikers. As will be seen on the trail, this is one of the best places in Lancashire for birdwatching, with wildfowl and waders out on the water and an impressive range of species attracted to woodland habitats. For more information about this and other trails, visit www.forestofbowland.com.

Worden Park

START Main car park, Worden
Lane, PR25 3DH, SD542210

DISTANCE 1½ miles (2.4km)

SUMMARY An easy walk
on surfaced paths

MAP OS Explorer 285
Southport & Chorley

WHERE TO EAT AND DRINK
The Coffee Shop in the courtyard

USEFUL WEBSITES
www.southribble.gov.uk;
www.brothersofcharity.org.uk

Situated on the southern edge of Leyland, Worden Park acts as a natural buffer
between town and countryside.

① The first part of the walk is not in the park at all but requires you
to return to Worden Lane and turn right, walking alongside the old
stone walls of the estate. Pass a second entrance and turn right onto a
footpath close by Swiss Lodge. You are now on the Shaw Brook Italian
Walk created for the Farington family, who once lived in the Hall.
In about 300yds you will reach the folly, which was built in the late
eighteenth century to adorn the small waterfall. It takes the form of an
arched ruin. Keep to the main path as it enters a more densely wooded
area and then crosses a wooden bridge. After a second footbridge there
is a stone shelter on a brow – at one time a summer house. The third
footbridge will bring you past a pond and onto a tarmac drive. Turn
right. A short distance ahead, turn right again onto a stoned path.

② When the path forks, bear right to reach the entrance to the
maze – a lime tree marks its centre. If you want to extend the walk by
5 miles, enter the maze. If not, turn right and walk along the outside of
the maze to reach the formal gardens. From here, there is easy access
into the courtyard and the Arts and Crafts centre and coffee shop.
Follow signs to return to the car park but, if you wish to extend your
walk, cross the playing fields to reach a wooded footpath beyond the
children's playground. Turn right to reach Worden Lane.

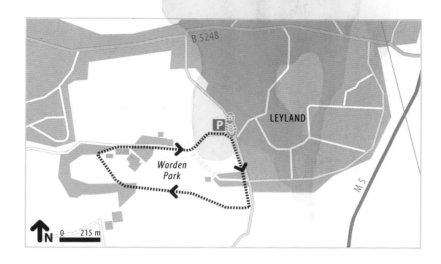

Points of interest

Once the home of the Farington family, Worden Park was taken over by the local authority in 1951. Since local government reorganization in 1974 it has been managed by South Ribble Borough Council. Covering over 60ha, it caters for a wide range of community activities. Since the inception of the Green Flag Award in 1996, Worden Park is the only open space north of London to be awarded it every year – a remarkable achievement.

The Dunsop Bridge Tramper Trail

START Dunsop Bridge village
car park, BB7 3BB, SD661501

DISTANCE Short route 1½ miles
(2.4km); long route 3 miles (4.8km)

SUMMARY Tramper Category 1.
Easy walking. There is one gate
to open so tramper users may
find it best to be accompanied

MAP OS Explorer OL41
Forest of Bowland

WHERE TO EAT AND DRINK
Puddleducks Café and Village Store,
www.puddleduckstearooms.co.uk,
T01200-448241

An accessible route in the heart of the Bowland Forest.

1 From the car park turn right on the road, walking towards the
eponymous bridge. Before you reach it, turn right onto a farm road
just after Puddleducks tea room and post office.

2 The road crosses a large pasture. After a children's playground on
the right, cross a cattle grid into the next field. Keep ahead towards
a terrace of cottages. Beyond the buildings enter woodland at a gate.
Now, close to the River Dunsop, keep ahead to a wooden bridge.

3 Now comes the moment of decision. After crossing the bridge,
turn left and a service road will take you back to Dunsop Bridge. After
a slight uphill climb the road descends to the main road opposite the
war memorial. However, if time allows, turn right at the bridge and
venture up the valley to reach in a mile and a half an impressive array
of utility buildings used to collect water.

4 This is a wonderful place to experience the heart of Bowland and
the country. Reaching the centre of Great Britain (see box) necessitates
a hike up to the top of Brennandale, the valley on the left. Given the
terrain, this expedition should not be undertaken in a tramper. From
here, retrace the outward route back to the footbridge and keep ahead
from there.

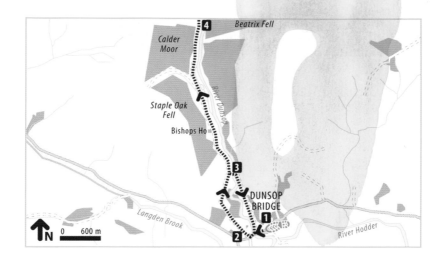

Points of interest

Some years ago the wizards at the Ordnance Survey decided upon the spot that represented the centre of the United Kingdom. Their answer turned out to be SD6418856541. This grid reference will put you on Whitendale Hanging Stones above Brennand Farm. The nearest settlement to this central location is Dunsop Bridge. BT sited its 100,000th public phone box especially in Dunsop Bridge to mark this special distinction. The phone box is opposite the car park.

The area has another distinction. HM The Queen once disclosed that if she were ever to retire she would choose this area of Lancashire to live. As Duke of Lancaster she would be very much on her estates, in the heart of her realm, in an Area of Outstanding Natural Beauty.

Rufford & Mere Sands Wood

START Mere Sands Wood visitors'
centre car park, L40 1TG, SD447160

DISTANCE Short route 1½ miles
(2.4km), accessible for wheelchairs;
long route 6 miles (9.7km)

SUMMARY Easy walking

MAP OS Explorer 285
Southport & Chorley

WHERE TO EAT AND DRINK
Fettler's Wharf, http://
fettlerswharfmarina.co.uk,
T01704-822888;
The Rufford Arms Hotel,
www.ruffordarms.com,
T01704-822040;
The Hesketh Arms, nearby on
the A59, T01704-821009

Mere Sands Wood, once a sand quarry, is now a local nature reserve managed
by Lancashire Wildlife Trust. This short walk involves a circuit of this splendid
amenity, while the longer route extends into the countryside nearby.

1 From the visitors' centre turn right and enter the woods on this
north-facing flank of the reserve. A broad path leads round to bring
you to a kissing gate at its south-east corner. Turn left through the gate
and exit the reserve. (For readers following the shorter walk, continue
on the main path as it turns westwards. The path is well signed and
will lead you back to the centre.)

2 The path soon passes the village cricket ground. Walking through
the residential area, you'll find the footpath will swap either side of
the sluice at each lane. At the first, Cousin's Lane, turn right across
the sluice and then left behind houses and continue with the water on
your left. This brings you to Brick Kiln Lane. Here, take a footpath to
the right of a chapel. On reaching Sluice Lane, cross to a footpath that
passes a large workshop and then bends round to the A59.

3 Turn right and then almost immediately left to cross a swing
bridge over the canal. Bear left to reach the towpath. With water on
your left, pass by a large marina and then the rear of Rufford Old Hall.

4 About 1½ miles after joining the canal, leave it at Spark Bridge
and the A581. Turn left and then left onto Spark Lane. Follow this

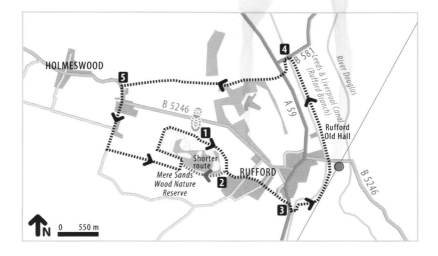

round to the A59 close to the Rufford Arms Hotel. Cross the road to Croston Dr, a private road but a public right of way. Until you reach Holmeswood the direction is west. At Woodbank join a track that skirts the property to its right. Beyond it, continue along a tarmac lane. After passing through a neck of woodland the lane bends to the left. Here, keep ahead on a footpath leading alongside large arable fields. Keep on the path for a little over 1,000yds until you reach the scattered community of Holmeswood.

⑤   On reaching Holmeswood Rd, turn left. Passing Mossend Farm, turn right onto Sandy Way. Continue along Sandy Way for over 600yds. Just before a low bridge crossing Rufford Boundary Sluice, turn left onto a footpath. This sluice will guide you back to Mere Sands Wood. After edging along arable fields, it joins a farm track and soon after enters the reserve. Follow signs back to the car park.

Points of interest

Rufford Old Hall (NT) was once home to the Hesketh family. There is credible evidence to suggest that Shakespeare performed here when his theatre company toured the north.

Caton Moor Tramper Trail

START Caton Moor Wind
Farm, LA2 9PR, SD570643

DISTANCE 1½ miles (2.4km)

SUMMARY Disabled
Ramblers Category 1

MAP OS Explorer OL41
Forest of Bowland

A superb location for a tramper trail, with stunning views across the Lune Valley
and out to Morecambe Bay.

1 Nearby at the picnic area there is a detailed information board
explaining about the wind farm and its contribution to energy supply.
Also, there is a brightly coloured directional marker. From the car
park it is necessary to drop back 50yds on the fell road to reach the
track leading to the wind farm. The track is composed of high quality
compacted aggregate for most of the route, apart for a short section of
compressed earth. The way leads past a white memorial stone erected
in memory of Anne Redferne, who was executed at Lancaster in 1612
as one of the so-called Pendle Witches. This is part of a number of
identical monuments erected around the district to mark the 400th
anniversary of the Witch Trials held in Lancaster. The track reaches a
gate – the only one on the route. After this it continues gently rising to
the highest part of the walk.

2 As the track swings right by turbine number 8 'Whinchat', there
are fine views across to Morecambe Bay and the Lake District beyond.
The track then swings right again in front of turbine number 7 'Fox'
and begins a slight climb over a spur before joining the outward route.

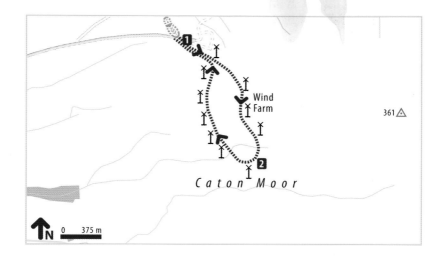

Points of interest

The wind farm at Caton is a particularly airy location with fine views. It is at once a wild and windy place and one connected with contemporary concerns about energy supply. It first came into service in 1994 at a time when there were only five other wind farms in the country. There are eight turbines on the site and each has been given a name by local primary school children. As far as the visitor is concerned, this is the only thing that distinguishes them (see www.tridos.co.uk for more information).

Calder Vale

START Calder Vale war memorial, PR3 1SH, SD530455

DISTANCE Short route 2 miles (3.2km); long route 3 miles (4.8km)

SUMMARY Mainly easy walking on lanes and farm tracks with a climb to Delph Lane across fields (on the long route)

MAP OS Explorer OL41 Forest of Bowland

A short walk from an industrial settlement, with a climb to a superb viewpoint.

1 From the war memorial head downhill into the old centre of the village. Cross the River Calder to reach The Square in front of the mill and Methodist chapel (alternate starting place at weekends). Bear left, passing Long Row on the right, to enter the woods on a footpath leading up to the church. The path quickly passes the old mill lodge with an attractive artificial lake on the right. After 500yds you will arrive at the rear gates of the churchyard. Keep ahead to pass the old school house to reach a junction. (During term time readers are asked to follow the concessionary path around to the right of the school playground to reach this point.)

2 Turn right. Now on an unsurfaced lane keep ahead past Lower Landskill Farm and then follow the farm road as it bends to the right, heading uphill with a wall to the right. In 200yds, after a cattle grid, arrive at a corner before the road turns right for Landskill Farm.

3 (Readers preferring the shorter walk can omit this part of the walk and resume directions described at 4 .) Turn left through a wooden gate onto a stony track leading uphill. This crosses two fields to reach Delph Lane. Turn right. After 500yds turn right onto a footpath accessed by the nearer of two wooden gates, close by the field corner. If it hasn't been already apparent, Delph Lane is surprisingly elevated so the view from this point is superlative, taking in the Lancashire Plain to the Fylde Coast. From the field corner bear right

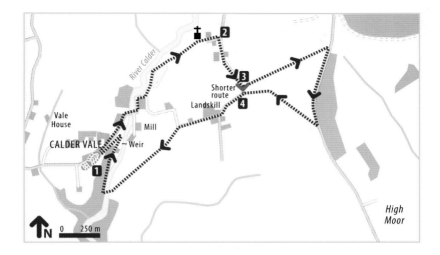

on a descent to a metal gate close to a small enclosed wood on the left. Enter the next field and continue downhill to the far right corner where you reach the farm track from Lower Landskill. Turn left.

④ Follow the track downhill to Landskill Farm. When you reach it, turn right through its yard. Ignore the path on the left to Cobble Hey and continue on a concrete track on the far side, passing the farmhouse on your right. After 200yds the track turns right. Here, take a footpath on the left through the left of two metal gates. Bearing right, cross pasture to reach and go through a wooden kissing gate and then continue on the same diagonal course to reach the River Calder. Cross the footbridge and turn right on a lane leading back to Calder Vale.

Points of interest

The first cotton mill was built here in 1835 and the remains of the old mill race that powered it are evident in the first part of the walk. Calder Vale was an industrial settlement – the old terraces put there to house the workers. The mill owners were Quakers so did not encourage alcohol, which is why the village does not possess a pub.

Cobble Hey Tramper Trail

START Cobble Hey Farm and
Gardens, PR3 0QN, SD545455

DISTANCE 2 miles (3km)

SUMMARY Tramper
Category 2, an easy walk

MAP OS Explorer OL41
Forest of Bowland

WHERE TO EAT AND DRINK The farm
is a popular visitor attraction and
has its own café (To1995-602643)

Here is another one of the many tramper trails across the county. As well as
providing access for those with disabilities, this route is a marvellous walk in its
own right.

① From the farmyard return to the drive. Immediately after the gate,
turn left onto a grassy track. Follow this with the gardens on the left
and begin to ascend Peacock Hill. As the track levels out, go through
a gate to arrive at a superb view point giving extensive views over
the Fylde.

② From the viewpoint continue to the next gate and, once through
it, bear left at a marker post. The trail drops gently to a wooden gate in
a fence, after which it crosses a large pasture to a wall. Turn right here
to climb to Delph Lane.

③ As you reach the lane, turn left through the gate into the
adjoining field. From the corner bear diagonally right to a gate in a
wall just above a small plantation. The right of way goes left here to a
gate in the opposite corner, but trampers should go straight across the
field. On the far side just before the wall, turn left onto a stony track
that leads down to the gate. Through the gate, turn left onto the farm
lane that leads down to the farm complex of Landskill.

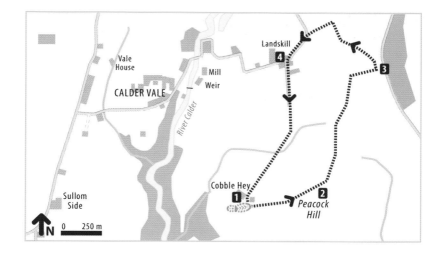

④ As you enter the farmyard, turn right and then left just before the farmhouse. This leads to a gate and a grassy track. Keep ahead past a birdwatchers' hide to a gate. Through this, follow the fence on the left and, where it bends, cross to a wooden gate on the left. Through this, turn right and keep ahead to where the path dips down to a brook and a metal gate. Go straight ahead to pick up a track, bringing you to the rear of the farm.

Further information

Not only does Cobble Hey have a tramper trail, it also has the use of a tramper. Please phone in advance if you wish to use it (see below). The Forest of Bowland AONB publishes a leaflet, *Wyresdale Wheels – Access for All*, which gives information about trails around Scorton. In addition, there are detailed trail routes, which are available at the Beacon Fell Visitor Centre or can be downloaded from www.forestofbowland.com. Note that the tramper trail uses concessionary footpaths as well as public rights of way. We suggest readers make a donation to the air ambulance service if going to Cobble Hey just to do the walk.

The Wyre Estuary Country Park

START Wyre Estuary Country
Park, FY5 5LR, SD356431

DISTANCE 2 miles (3.2km)

SUMMARY Easy

MAP OS Explorer 296 Lancaster,
Morecambe & Fleetwood

WHERE TO EAT AND DRINK
The Visitors' Centre Café

USEFUL WEBSITE
www.wyre.gov.uk for details
of the County Park

A gentle exploration of one of Lancashire's most popular country parks.

① From the visitors' centre go straight ahead on the left side of
the car park to pick up the Wyreside Trail. In quick succession this
passes a bus stop, picnic tables and a family area. At the drive the
trail divides. Cross the drive to join the riverside path close to the
salt marsh.

② Follow the path for the next mile as it hugs the shore, turning
east to a small creek. After passing beneath electricity pylons, the
path reaches the Cockle Hall picnic area. Beyond this the path begins
a gentle swing round to the right to a path junction. This feature is
known locally as Ramper Pot.

③ Turn right through a gate to follow a path between high hedges
as it bends left to join Underbank Rd. Turn right. Follow the road to
Stanah House Farm and follow it left as it continues as Stanah Rd to
reach River Rd. Turn right; River Rd leads back to the Country Park.

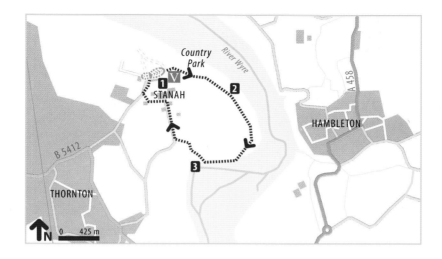

Points of interest

The Wyre Estuary is an area rich in birdlife, its mudflats attracting waders and waterfowl at low tide. The Country Park is a popular amenity providing an outdoor space for local people and visitors alike. The Countryside Service maintains a network of paths on both sides of the river between Shard Bridge and Fleetwood. The route described is a good introduction to the area and is one of many, details of which can be picked up at the centre.

It would be easy to mistake the area of higher land to the right as you start the walk as just a low hill. It is in fact a drumlin – a morainic deposit composed mainly of boulder clay left by a sheet of receding ice. Drumlins tend to be elongated, somewhat like a half-buried egg. If these finer geological points are lost on you, perhaps you could climb to the top of it instead and enjoy the view. Use the footpath to the right, close to the Cockle Hall picnic area.

START Cuerden Valley Park, Lower Kem Mill car park (pay & display), PR6 7EA, SD575217

DISTANCE 2 miles (3.2km)

SUMMARY Easy walking on well-maintained paths and cycle track

MAP OS Explorer 285 Southport & Chorley

WHERE TO EAT AND DRINK The Bobbin Mill, a Marston's house further along Dawson's Lane towards the A49 (www.bobbinmillpub.co.uk, T01772 458160)

USEFUL WEBSITES www.curdenvalleypark.org.uk; www.brothersofcharity.org.uk; www.buckshaw.org

This short walk starts in Cuerden Valley Park but soon climbs to a remarkable viewpoint overlooking Buckshaw village, before returning along a newly created cycle route.

[1]   On the left side of the car park from the entrance, take a footpath close to a reminder about paying and displaying. This quickly leads uphill between fields to Lisieux Hall. This is the Lancashire home of the Brothers of Charity.

[2]   The path turns left and goes through the wood just before the hall and edges round to the visitors' car park. Here, cross the main drive to follow a narrow lane with the complex on the right.

[3]   When you reach Dawson Lane, cross the road on the corner (taking care with the traffic) to a track opposite. Though there is no sign to indicate it, you have just entered Buckshaw village. Where the track divides we suggest you take the left fork and, after this reaches a brow, turn right onto a grassy path that soon arrives at the first of two viewpoints. Continue 250yds further on to the second and higher viewpoint – one of the finest viewpoints in this part of Lancashire. Nearby is the village itself. This is one of the largest development sites of its kind in the north of England. Return to Dawson Lane by way of a track leading down to the left as you retrace your steps along the hill.

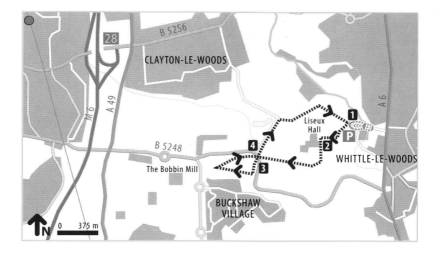

④ Cross the road and take the lane back onto Brothers of Charity land but this time turn left onto the tarmac cycle track. This track takes you through farmland that surrounds Lisieux Hall and drops down into Cuerden Valley Park. As you reach the main path, turn right for the car park.

Points of interest

Lisieux Hall is the Lancashire base of the Brothers of Charity. Founded in Belgium in 1807 by Canon Peter Triest, this religious order worked to provide care and support for the poor, the aged and the disabled. The foundation now has a worldwide mission. In Lancashire Brothers of Charity services have been supporting people with learning disabilities since 1930.

START Bus shelter, centre of
Great Eccleston, opposite the
White Bull, PR3 0ZB, SD427402

DISTANCE 2½ miles (4km)

SUMMARY Easy

MAP OS Explorer 296 Lancaster,
Morecambe & Fleetwood

WHERE TO EAT AND DRINK
The Courtyard Caffé,
www.thecourtyardcaffebar.co.uk,
T01995-672011;
The White Bull T01995-670203;
The Black Bull, T01995-670224;
The Cartford Inn,
www.thecartfordinn.co.uk,
T01995-670116

The River Wyre is the longest river to flow entirely within Lancashire. This
walk follows a large loop along its raised embankment close to the village of
Great Eccleston.

[1] Cross High Street, turn right and then almost immediately left
on a side street that passes the public toilets. After 100yds turn right
onto Back Lane. Keep on this to where it bends to the right. Turn left
on a public footpath, which leads down on a concrete track to the
A586 Garstang Rd. Cross with care to reach a wooden kissing gate
to the right of a farm. Through this, go through a metal gate almost
opposite and bear right to the far corner of the field. Cross a stile and
then, following a fence on the right, reach another stile before the
embankment. Climb up the slope and join the river.

[2] Turn left. The route now follows a hairpin bend in the river as it
sweeps round towards Cartford Bridge. After 600yds, close to White
Hall on the opposite bank, the path passes a metal footbridge and
pipeline. In another 1,000yds it draws close to Cartford Toll Bridge.

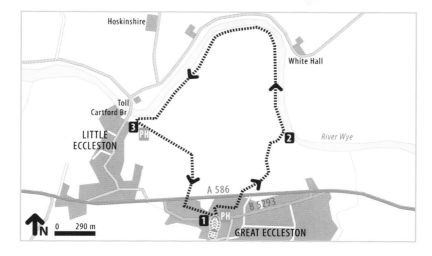

③ As the embankment ends, and before reaching the Cartford Arms car park, turn left over a small ladder stile and turn left. Follow the path to a footbridge over a ditch and then continue to a stile in the right corner of the next field. This leads onto a farm track (Butt's Lane). Turn right. Keep on this past the large paddock to the right to reach Garstang Rd. Cross with care and continue on Butt's Lane to its junction with Back Lane. Turn left. In 200yds turn right to return to the start.

Points of interest

Great Eccleston is a bustling village with a weekly market and an annual agricultural show. Featured in the show is the event of tractor-pulling. The large paddock passed on Butt's Lane is a purpose-built arena for the North West Tractor Pullers Club (see www.nwtpc.co.uk).

Entwistle & Wayoh Reservoir

START United Utilities Batridge Barn car park, Turton & Entwistle Reservoir, BL7 0EW (nearby), SD721172

DISTANCE Short route 2½ miles (4km); long route 5 miles (8km)

SUMMARY Short route very easy shoreline amble; long route more undulating than the short route but not hard

MAP OS Explorer 287 West Pennine Moors

WHERE TO EAT AND DRINK The Strawbury Duck, www.thestrawburyduck.co.uk, T01204-852013

These walks follow the shorelines of two delightful reservoirs. As well as being suitable for the whole family, the abundance of waterfowl provides an added attraction.

1️⃣ From the car park drop down to the south corner of the reservoir and the shoreline track. Turn left. You are now on a section of the Witton Weavers Way. With the reservoir on your right, follow the track. After 10mins the reservoir narrows into a long arm with Fox Hill Plantation on the opposite shore.

2️⃣ At the end of the reservoir cross the wooden bridge over a feeder stream and turn right. The path hugs the shore below the densely planted conifers of Fox Hill. After an inlet heralded by 'The Wader', an ornamental piece of artwork in the shape of a heron, the route reaches the widest expanse of the reservoir.

3️⃣ In a little under 600yds after the inlet, turn left on a path going up through the trees. The short walk continues 300yds along the shore, and turns right onto a service road that crosses the dam end of the reservoir. This will quickly return you to the car park. For those readers wishing to follow the longer walk, take the footpath as it climbs to a more substantial track (Edge Lane). Turn right. This leads to the Strawbury Duck and Entwistle. Turn left.

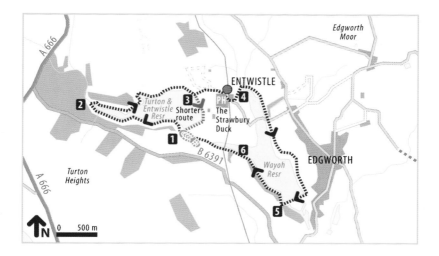

4 Cross the railway bridge and follow the lane as it swings right. In a little over 50yds take a footpath on the left leading downhill to woods. Keep on this path and soon you will come to the north end of Wayoh Reservoir. After crossing two footbridges, bear right on the main path and soon, in sight of water, keep ahead to reach the causeway at Hob Lane. Keep ahead over the lane to follow the eastern shore of the main basin of Wayoh Reservoir. To the left pastureland opens up below Isherwood Fold. After passing by a conifer plantation the path climbs through gorse into meadows before dropping down to the dam end of the reservoir. Cross to the far side and turn right.

5 Follow the shoreline for 800yds until you reach the causeway.

6 Bear left. The path leads below the railway viaduct to climb up through woods to reach the car park.

START Avenham Lane
entrance, Avenham Park,
Preston, PR1 8JT, SD538289

DISTANCE 2½ miles (4km)

SUMMARY Easy. Suitable for
pushchairs, wheelchairs and walkers
who prefer not to do stiles.

MAP OS Explorer 286
Blackpool & Preston

WHERE TO EAT AND DRINK
The Pavilion Café,
www.avenhampark.org,
T01772-907740

This walk starts in Avenham Park and quickly enters Miller Park – two of
Preston's most attractive open spaces – before crossing the Ribble for a circuit
through a local nature reserve.

1 From the main entrance descend on the main drive, branching
right just after the chalet on a broad walkway. To the right is a war
memorial to the Boer War; to the left the Japanese Gardens. Pass
beneath the old East Lancashire railway line to enter Miller Park. Laid
out in a more formal style than its neighbour, the walkway with its
balustrade acts like a gallery over the features of the park – fountain,
flowerbeds and bandstand. Pass the statue of the Earl of Derby and
keep ahead until just before the embankment of the West Coast
railway line. Here, bear left on a path taking you through a grotto-like
archway and descend to the riverside beneath the imposing viaduct.

2 Turn left and follow the riverside walk back beneath the viaduct
into Avenham Park. Turn immediately left and then climb the stairs
to the top of the embankment (for wheels there is ramp further on).
Cross the river, passing into the borough of South Ribble and Preston
Junction local nature reserve. Keep on the broad path for 500yds
and then follow it left as is drops to a track. Cross the track to regain
the top of the embankment. Here is a particularly good viewing
point both for Preston to the north and the playing fields of Cardinal
Newman College to the south. Keep ahead to where the path meets
the Old Tram Rd.

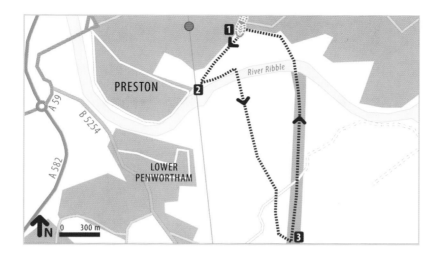

③ Turn left. The walk now returns to Preston along a magnificent avenue of trees. This was the route of a tramway that once served to connect the Leeds–Liverpool Canal with Preston. Now it is a popular amenity for walkers, runners and cyclists. Not until you are close to the river do you break out into the open to cross the Old Tram Bridge. On the far side keep ahead to climb through barriers to reach a broad open space in front of the Belvedere, an attractive stone building. Here it is worth a short diversion to the right, first to admire Avenham House, the Italianate Victorian house overlooking the park, and then to look at the Sebastopol cannons, trophies from the Crimean War. Near them is a viewpoint over the River Ribble that is one of Preston's finest. From the Belvedere keep ahead on an upper path, with the main bowl of the park down to the left. This will return you to the entrance.

Aitken Wood

START Barley village car park and picnic site, BB12 9JX, SD823403

DISTANCE 3 miles (4.8km)

SUMMARY Mainly easy but with a steep climb into the wood to reach the start of the trail. The upper part of the trail is accessible for tramper-type vehicles; these can be booked in advance (48hrs notice) from the Bowland Experience, T01200-446553

MAP OS Explorer OL41 Forest of Bowland

WHERE TO EAT AND DRINK
The Barley Village Tearoom, T01282-694127;
The Pendle Inn, www.pendle-inn.co.uk, T01282-614808

USEFUL WEBSITES
www.visitpendle.com;
www.lancashirewitches400.org

A fabulous family walk, following the Pendle Sculpture Trail through conifer woodland. For full appreciation of the sculptures be sure to have a copy of the leaflet produced by Pendle Council.

①   From the car park take the path behind the information centre and café, crossing a wedge of parkland to a footbridge leading onto Barley's main street – The Bullion. Turn right. Continue along the Bullion and, soon after the Methodist church, turn right on a tarmac service road in the direction of Blacko. This lane soon becomes unsurfaced as it approaches the lower of the two Black Moss Reservoirs. Incidentally, there is a particularly fine view of Pendle Hill across the water along this stretch. At the end of Lower Black Moss, bear right at a junction to make a short gentle ascent to the level of the upper reservoir. It's a further 200yds to the entrance to Aitken Wood on the right.

②   Even without the Sculpture Trail this would be a worthwhile walk, providing superb views of the countryside on the east side of Pendle Hill. As the track turns right it begins to climb with surprising steepness as it enters the wood. After 300yds the way begins to level out as it reaches a junction. The recommended route starts from this

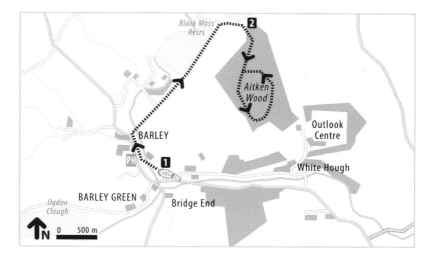

point on a circuit of half a mile, in an anti-clockwise direction. Before reaching the southern edge of the wood, the trail swings left and then loops back on a downward track to the junction. From here, if you are satisfied you have seen all that there is to see, retrace your steps to Barley.

Points of interest

The predominant theme of the Pendle Sculpture Trail is based upon events that took place nearby over 400 years ago. Following what nowadays might be regarded as a domestic dispute between neighbours, the subsequent investigation identified a group of eight women and two men to be witches. They were sent to Lancaster for trial, found guilty and executed. Sarah McDade's ceramic plaques waymark the route as you follow it through the wood. Interspersed with these are the tree sculptures of Philippe Handford, Steve Blaylock's metal bats, owl and giant spider's web representing the natural world after dark, and 'The Witchfinder' a statue by Martyn Bednarczuk that reminds us of the role of Roger Nowell, the local magistrate who extracted 'confessions' from the accused.

START Denny Beck car park, Halton, LA2 9HQ, SD503645

DISTANCE 3 miles (4.8km)

SUMMARY Easy

MAP OS Explorer OL41 Forest of Bowland

WHERE TO EAT AND DRINK There is a tea bar at the Crook O' Lune car park (weekends only Nov–Easter)

This route explores both sides of the River Lune between Halton and the Crook O' Lune.

1 From the car park return to the lane, turn right and cross the River Lune on Bulk Bridge. At the far side turn right into Mill Lane. As you approach a modern three-storey housing development, bear right. Keep ahead and then, as you approach an old workshop, bear right on a track soon leading past a modern terrace of houses with the river on the right. At this point you are just downstream from Halton Weir and close to the site of a long-demolished mill. Close to the weir the route climbs the wooded embankment and then follows a narrow path through meadows. As it approaches a wide bend in the river, it enters woods to climb to Low Rd. Exit the woods by a kissing gate and cross to a walled path opposite. Turn right. Keep to the roadside path, which will quickly bring you to the rear of Crook O' Lune car park.

2 The particular geography of this location on the great hairpin bend of the river can be confusing for the first-time visitor. At the far end of the car park do not drop to the broad cycleway that crosses the Lune on the old railway bridges, as it will take you back to the car park when you turn right (unless you are short of time, of course). Instead, turn left onto Low Rd and cross by the road bridge. On the far side the road bends to the right. After this, take a riverside footpath through a metal gate, which after passing through a picnic area enters woodland. This soon climbs up towards the busy A683 Kirkby Lonsdale Rd before dropping back to the river to pass beneath the old railway bridge

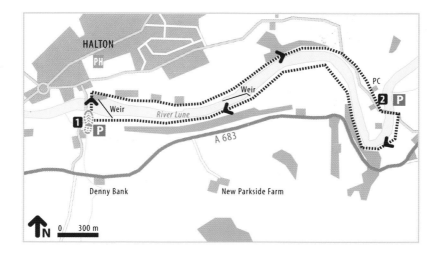

carrying the cycleway. Soon after this the path reaches broad fields. Keep ahead until the path comes close to the weir and then follow it left as it climbs up to join the cycleway. Turn right for the car park.

Points of interest

The River Lune Millennium Riverside Park is an 8-mile stretch of the river from Salt Ayre to Caton, passing through the city of Lancaster. To the south of the river the route of an old railway has now been converted to a cycleway and forms part of the National Cycle Network. This makes it accessible for wheelchairs and prams as well as bikes. On the north side of the river the Lune Valley long-distance path passes through the park, linking Kirkby Lonsdale to Lancaster.

START Car park just before
Hornby Bridge on A683,
Hornby, LA2 8JR, SD584683

DISTANCE 3 miles (4.8km)

SUMMARY Mainly easy walking
by the riverside or across fields

MAP OS Explorer OL41
Forest of Bowland

WHERE TO EAT AND DRINK
The Castle Inn,
www.thecastleinnhornby.co.uk,
T01254-222279;
The Royal Oak,
www.thwaitespub.co.uk,
T01524-221228;
Hornby Post Office and
Tearooms, T01524-221237

A lovely riverside walk with fine views of the Yorkshire Dales.

① From the car park turn left onto the main road and cross the
bridge. At the far end turn left onto a footpath tucked tightly by the
corner of the bridge. At first the path takes you through woodland
before crossing a stile into open fields. Keep ahead along the banks of
the River Wenning to its meeting with the Lune. About 15mins from
Hornby you will come to the confluence.

② With the river on your left, walk up to Loyn Bridge. At first the
way is flat, but after Priory Farm the route becomes more undulating
as you near the bridge. The path enters woodland (bedecked with
bluebells in spring). Some 100yds before you reach Loyn Bridge, take
a concessionary path on the right to the lane. The path rises steeply
from the river.

③ Turn right onto Fleet Lane. When you arrive at the road junction
with the A683, turn right for the village centre.

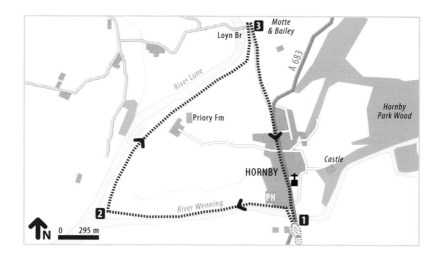

Points of interest

Hornby Castle, a privately owned grade 1 listed building, perches above the village and can best be seen from the bridge. Built originally for the Neville family in the thirteenth century, the castle has undergone numerous restorations. The present building mainly dates from the middle of the nineteenth century.

The most obvious and striking feature of St Margaret's Parish Church is its octagonal tower, commissioned by Sir Edward Stanley, the then occupant of the castle at the start of the sixteenth century. It was reputed to be an act of thanksgiving on his safe return from the battle of Flodden Field in 1513.

Yarrow Valley Country Park

START The Visitors' Centre
and Café, off Birkacre Rd,
Chorley, PR7 3QL, SD570152

DISTANCE 3 miles (4.8km)

SUMMARY Easy

MAP OS Explorer 285
Southport & Chorley

WHERE TO EAT AND DRINK
The Treeface Café inside the
visitors' centre, T01257-279767

USEFUL WEBSITE www.chorley.gov.uk

A walk along the River Yarrow as it winds its way to the south-west of Chorley.

1 The first part of the route follows the River Yarrow upstream towards Duxbury. From the visitors' centre turn left and climb a flight of steps to Big Lodge (there is a wheelchair access point further to the left). With the water on your right, follow the path to its far end as it joins the path by the River Yarrow. Turn left. Keep ahead, passing a small lodge on the left, and enter woodland, soon reaching a weir with its fish ladder (this is as far as wheelchairs can go.) Climb a short flight of steps and continue walking upstream. After passing the remains of an old coalmine shaft, keep ahead then bear left where the footpath cuts across a bend in the river to a footbridge.

2 Cross the bridge and continue with the river on your left. After passing through woodlands the path crosses a metal bridge and then climbs slightly to exit the woods by a wooden kissing gate. Cross pasture and then drop to a wooden footbridge across the Yarrow once more in woods. Take the left track (less used than the main track), which leads to a steep embankment. Climb this, aided by a long flight of steps, to reach a stile. Cross onto a track passing a property on the right.

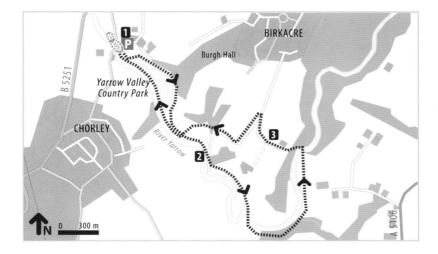

③ After passing a farm entrance the track turns to the right, climbing up to a junction. Turn sharp left onto a track leading back towards the valley. Turn right 200yds further on at a junction as the track passes through a patch of woodland to reach a metal gate. Continue over a wide meadow to enter the riverside woods, soon arriving back at the outward path. Turn right. The way back to the centre is straight ahead, taking the path between the river and Big Lodge.

Points of interest

The Yarrow Valley is another of Lancashire's excellent country parks, with a ranger service and full programme of events appealing to all age groups of the community it serves. Close to the visitors' centre there is an excellent history trail, most of which is wheelchair/pushchair-friendly. This area of the country park was once a hive of industry. There were collieries, forges, bleach works and mills. This accounts for the need of the lodges – the reservoirs that helped to harness water power. Richard Arkwright set up a textile mill close to where the visitors' centre is today. In 1779 a large mob burnt the mill down, driven by the fear that the factory system would deprive them of their livelihoods. After that, Arkwright concentrated his efforts at Cromford in Derbyshire.

Downham

START Downham village visitors' car park, BB7 4BS, SD784441

DISTANCE 3½ miles (5.6km)

SUMMARY Mainly easy

MAP OS Explorer OL41 Forest of Bowland

WHERE TO EAT AND DRINK
Village post office, shop and tearoom, T01200-441242

USEFUL WEBSITE
www.downhamvillage.org.uk

A delightful circuit from one of Lancashire's most attractive villages.

① From the car park turn right onto West Lane and almost immediately right onto a footpath. After a gate the path leads across fields at first, with the fence line on the right. After passing Longlands Wood (also to the right) go through a kissing gate leading into a wide meadow. Here, bear slightly left to pick up a waymarked fence end and then continue to a kissing gate in a corner. Through this, keep ahead in the next field, aiming towards the end of Worsaw Hill. After a kissing gate the path follows a stone wall on the left. Just before Worsaw End House, turn left through a metal gate near the end of the wall and cross diagonally left to pick up a farm drive. Follow this to its junction with West Lane.

② Turn left and then right onto a farm lane, which leads up to Barkerfield Farm. At the farm follow the lane as it bends left towards Hookcliffe, a large farm complex about 300yds beyond Barkerfield. Where the track bears left towards the main buildings go through a kissing gate to the right of a wooden gate to follow a broad, grassy track below the open fellside. After the next gate the track ceases to be grassy – keep on it until it brings you to Pendle Rd. Turn right and keep on the road for 200yds, before turning left onto a footpath opposite a small car park.

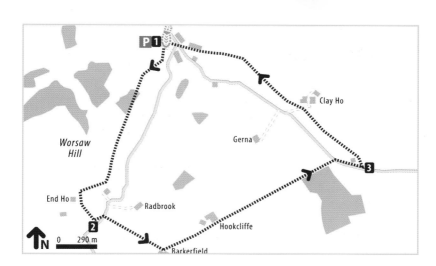

③ The path soon leads steeply down into a gully before climbing up left to a broad grassy shelf close to a stone barn and a pair of benches (a more inviting place for a picnic we do not know!). Cross a stone stile in the wall below the barn and keep ahead close to the right fence line to cross a large pasture to its far right corner. Continue in the same direction, crossing the drive of Clay House (to the right), and after a footbridge keep ahead to the broad meadows close to Downham Beck on the right. The village hall on a prominent rise provides a good aiming point. Follow the stream to reach the edge of Downham village. As you reach the main street, turn left for the car park.

Points of interest

Little has changed in the village of Downham over the past few centuries. In 1961 it was used as the main location for the film *Whistle Down the Wind*, starring Bernard Lee, Alan Bates and Hayley Mills.

Ormskirk

START Hants Lane car park
(pay & display), Burscough St,
Ormskirk, L39 2EL, SD415485

DISTANCE 3½ miles (5.6km)

SUMMARY Easy walk combining
town and countryside

MAP OS Explorer 285
Southport & Chorley

WHERE TO EAT AND DRINK In
the town centre; there are too
many to list here but all tastes
and pockets are catered for.

A fascinating walk, exploring the history and nearby countryside of Ormskirk.

[1] The first part of the walk visits the attractive town centre and
parish church. From the car park return to Burscough St and turn
right. Pass the handsome porticoes of the Old Dispensary and
the library to cross Derby St, and continue along pedestrianized
Burscough St, a conservation area. At the Clock Tower turn right into
Church St and walk up to the A570 and cross to the parish church.

[2] The church is a rewarding place to visit if open. On leaving the
church, turn right onto the A570 Park St and follow the road round
past Coronation Park and the war memorial. Continue past Morrisons
and cross the railway to reach the intersection at St Helen's Rd. Here,
cross the road at traffic islands to reach Victoria Park on the corner of
Ruff Lane.

[3] Exit the park by its top left corner onto Ruff Lane and turn right.
The route passes the old grammar school on the left (now converted
into apartments) and the University of Edge Hill on the right. It also
enters the Ruff Lane conservation area. As the lane opens out with the
main campus down to the right, cross to enter Ruff Wood local nature
reserve. Bear right on a broad path taking you across to Vicarage Lane.

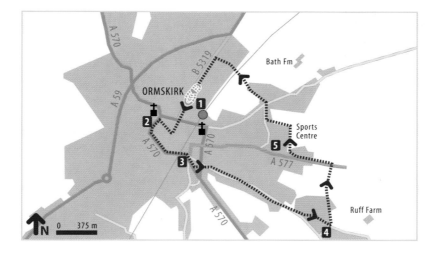

④ If you wish to extend the walk by a mile, exit the wood here and keep on Vicarage Lane to St James's Church, an attractive nineteenth-century building, returning to this corner of the wood. Take the footpath left and cross the wood, passing the old sandstone quarry at its heart. Keep ahead to an exit taking you onto a broad field. Cross this on a footpath to Wigan Rd (A577). Turn left. Walk past Ormskirk School on the right and at traffic lights turn right into Thompson Av.

⑤ Follow Thompson Av. Keep on it as it bends sharply to the right just before the school playing fields. As the road nears a junction, turn right onto a ginnel leading to a field. This will provide the best view of the Victorian water tower. Retrace your steps to Thompson Av and turn right into Tower Hill. At the next junction turn left and then right into Waterworks Rd. Pass the primary school on the left and turn right onto a cycle path between houses. Keep on this as it leads to fields on the edge of the town. Across to the right a rather distinctive building will be seen. This is Bath Lodge, an eighteenth-century folly recently restored as a residence and featured in Channel 4's *Restoration Man*. Keep ahead under the railway and pass through a commercial estate to Burscough St. Turn left for the car park.

24 | Clougha Pike

START Birk Bank car park, Rigg
Lane, near Quernmore, LA2
9EH (nearby), SD526603

DISTANCE 4 miles (6.4km)

SUMMARY Strenuous. From Windy
Clough to the summit is a steep
climb involving scrambling at times.
Good map and compass skills are
essential in misty conditions

MAP OS Explorer OL41
Forest of Bowland

A thrilling ascent of one of Bowland's finest hills.

1 From the car park go through the wooden gate leading onto the
fellside. On a broad grassy track keep ahead, and when it forks in
200yds bear right and then follow it as it curves to the right. At a metal
gate turn left, dropping down onto duckboards which cross a section
of marshy ground. After these, follow the obvious track through
scattered trees gently upwards to a wall. When you reach two ladder
stiles, do not cross but turn left. The path climbs up towards the rocky
nab that is the end of Windy Clough. As the path levels out, turn right
onto a narrower path to reach the nab. Continue north-eastwards on a
faint path along the edge of the ridge to the right of a wall. As you near
the far end of the ridge, drop down through a thicket to reach a gate in
a wall in the valley.

2 After passing through the gate, follow a narrow path beside the
wall – not always easy to pick out as you negotiate the shattered rock.
The way is steep and rocky, climbing almost 500ft to reach the summit
plateau with the wall on the right. After an initial stretch taking you
over the lip of Little Windy Clough, the path continues close to the
wall and finally levels out amidst peat and heather. Further along
the ridge to the south-east the summit will come into view. Bearing
right, the path leads round to a gate in the wall and then crosses open
moorland, cutting a corner to another wooden gate. (At the time
of writing and for the foreseeable future there is a large gap in the

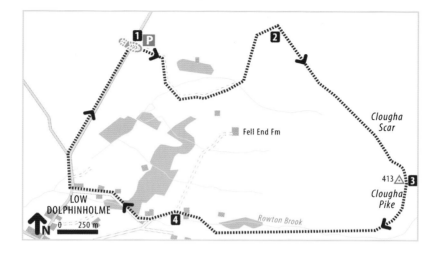

wall to the right of the gate.) Beyond this, turn right to complete the final ascent, passing a prominent cairn before finally arriving at the trig point.

③ Compared to the climb, everything else about the walk becomes easy. Leading briefly south from the summit, a peaty path begins to drop and swing westwards, swapping heather for sedge as it makes its descent. Although not waymarked it is broad and clear, taking you across Rowton Brook and then dropping to the fields above Rooten Brook Farm. About 20–30mins of descent will bring you to the track leading back over the brook and into the farm.

④ Keep ahead through the farm and continue along its drive. After the lane swings left, bear right onto a footpath leading past a large property. The track leads down to open fields. Keep ahead to follow a wall to the yard of Old Mill House. Turn left onto its drive. When you reach the road, turn right. In 200yds turn right onto Rigg Lane. The car park is 800yds along this road.

START Goldacre Lane, car
park on the left immediately
after a track/bridleway, BB6
7UT (nearby), SD724332

DISTANCE 4 miles (6.4km)

SUMMARY An easy walk
with two moderate climbs
and one steep descent

MAP OS Explorer 287
West Pennine Moors

Here is a landscape of surprise and unexpectedness, overlooked by visitors to
the county, but most rewarding when explored on foot.

① Turn left out of the car park onto Goldacre Lane. After the lane
bends to the right you will reach Shawcliff cottage. Ignore the footpath
sign directing you up a track and after 150yds look for a wooden stile
on the left. Cross this and climb steeply towards and over a stile in
the wall. Cross the track and a stile nearly opposite – then turn left
along a less distinct path. On this section, with the steep side of Sunny
Bank on your right and surrounded by gorse, you may feel somewhat
enclosed, but soon you reach a more open prospect. The path leads
across fields to the north-east corner of Dean Clough reservoir. When
you reach the wall, turn right to commence a short ascent with a
wall on your left. Keep following the wall, ignoring a wooden gate
and stile with waymarker, until you arrive at a metal gate. Following
the waymarkers, cross both the stile next to it and the next stile to
reach the highest point on the grassy path beyond. Here you will be
rewarded with a grand view of the Ribble Valley. More immediately,
the village of York will be a short way in front of you.

② On reaching York Rd turn left, pass the Lord Nelson and leave the
village. Keep on the road for a little under 500yds.

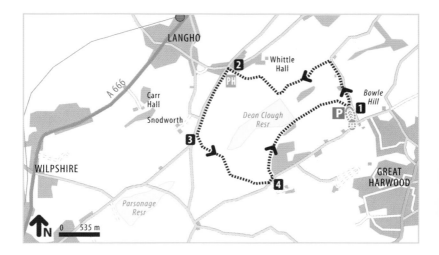

③ Pass a road to the right and then cross the stile at the first footpath sign on the left. Bear slightly right, crossing the field to reach a stile in the wall. Cross the stile and walk on a steep path downhill, aiming for the tip of the reservoir. You may be tempted to continue on the track, hugging this shore of the reservoir, but your way is up, beside a ditch on a faint path. When you reach a broad track, turn left and this will lead you to Harwood Rd.

④ Turn left. Walk along the road towards Great Harwood. Just before a conifer plantation turn left onto a grassy track. Follow the track downhill towards Dean Clough Reservoir. Beyond a kissing gate the track peters out to become a narrow footpath. Descend with a plantation on your right. As the path levels out you come to the first of a pair of kissing gates with a wall on the left. Some 100–150yds before the gate at the end of the track, look for the newly created tarmac path through kissing gates. Take this and the track leads to the bridleway that brings you back to Goldacre Lane and the car park.

START By the village hall, Hurst Green, BB7 9JQ, SD684379

DISTANCE 4 miles (6.4km)

SUMMARY Easy

MAP OS Explorer 287 West Pennine Moors

WHERE TO EAT AND DRINK
The Shireburn Arms Hotel, www. shireburnarmshotel.co.uk, T01254-826678; The Eagle and Child, www.eagleandchildhurstgreen. co.uk, T01254-826207

This short walk explores the village, the grounds of Stonyhurst College and some of the nearby countryside.

① Turn left out of the car park and follow the road down to the war memorial. Opposite the memorial follow The Warren to its end and then take the footpath, following the wall on the left. Through a kissing gate follow the path, keeping the hedge on the left. When the path reaches a path junction, turn right. After passing through a metal kissing gate, keep the hedge on the left. After a second kissing gate the path dips down between woods on the left and playing fields on the right to bring you to Stonyhurst College itself, close to the chapel. Turn left. The right of way crosses the main entrance, with the drive and ornamental ponds on the left. Keep ahead, passing college houses on the left, to arrive at a lane. Turn left.

② After passing Stockbridge Cottages on the left, you will reach the drive of Higher Deer House, also on the left, its public footpath sign somewhat concealed by foliage in the summer. Walk down the farm track for 800yds and through the farm (aided by yellow waymark arrows), taking a footpath across a field over a stile in a fence to Deer House Wood. Drop down to Dean Brook, cross the footbridge and climb the steep-sided valley to reach a fence. Cross this. The path edges around the wood and, after a ladder stile, reaches a stile in a wall. Cross onto a broad farm track. From this point you may wish

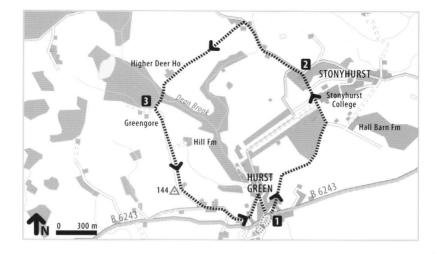

to take a short detour to admire the former royal hunting lodge of Greengore, a little way to the right.

③ The route now turns left and follows the track as it bends to the right. Keep on this as it reaches tarmac on its descent towards the village. After 600yds at New House look for a stile in the hedge on the right. Over this, it is an easy 1min stroll to the trig point on Doe Hill for a wonderful 360-degree view. Returning to the farm road, after 900yds turn left when you reach a lane. After 250yds this brings you round to a lane leading to the rear of the church. Sugi-san's memorial is not far from this entrance (see box). Follow the lane down a pretty dell and then up into the village. Turn right to return to the start.

Points of interest

In the quiet churchyard of St John the Evangelist, Hurst Green, there is a striking obelisk memorial dedicated to one Ikutaro Sugi, a 'Japanese Subject' who died in October 1905 at the age of thirty. He was an 'assistant commissioner in the Chinese Imperial Maritime Customs'. It is thought he had some connection with Stonyhurst College.

Longridge Fell

START Quarry car park, Clitheroe Old Rd, PR3 2YU (nearby), SD665397

DISTANCE 4 miles (6.4km)

SUMMARY Moderate

MAPS OS Explorer 287 West Pennine Moors and OS Explorer OL41 Forest of Bowland

The dense plantations of larch that once covered Longridge Fell have been much reduced in recent years by disease, but there are still enough trees to allow the walker to enjoy this upland.

1 From the car park turn right and continue along Clitheroe Old Rd towards – well, Clitheroe! In a little under 200yds turn left onto a footpath. Until the recent past this area was densely covered with tall conifers; not anymore. Keep on the path as it leads to a brook in 350yds and then continues alongside a fence, beyond which the fields of Green Thorn Farm come into view. Keep on the path as it leads up through trees to skirt the farm and then climb behind it to reach another cleared area. In a little under 400yds from the farm you arrive at a broad forestry track. Cross this to follow the path up a firebreak between stands of trees. When you reach a second forestry track bear right, crossing it to take the first path on the left.

2 Follow this narrow path through the dense plantation. After a few minutes the path reaches a broken wall, crosses it, and then immediately turns left to follow the wall upwards through trees. This is the most arduous section of the walk, but it is worth every effort when the open fellside is reached. Step over a stone stile in a wall on the right and walk towards the trig point some 300yds further along. On a clear day the views are magnificent – all yours and no charge. Now commences a long descent. Continue along the ridge with the wall on the left.

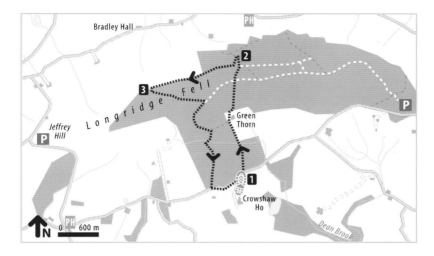

(3) Turn left 350yds from the trig point to cross the wall by a stone stile and walk across the track to a wire fence. A footpath immediately forks in front of you. Take the left fork. Through trees you arrive quickly at the terminus of a forest track. Follow the track as it sweeps downwards. On reaching a junction turn right. Trees give way to cleared ground and more extensive views, before arriving at a barrier gate that leads onto the road. Turn left for the car park.

START Close to the Highwayman
Inn, Nether Burrow, LA6 2RJ,
SD614751. Parking is a problem
here – apart from the car park of the
Highwayman – but the route is on the
Lancaster–Kirkby Lonsdale (No. 81B)
bus service, which is fairly regular

DISTANCE 4 miles (6.4km)

SUMMARY Easy. The section
of road at the start and end of
the walk has no pavement

MAP OS Explorer OL2 Yorkshire
Dales, Southern & Western areas

WHERE TO EAT AND DRINK
The Highwayman,
www.thehighwayman.co.uk,
T01524-273338

This short walk gives you lovely views of the hills of the Yorkshire Dales without
too much effort.

1   From the inn car park turn right in the direction of Kirkby
Lonsdale. After 300yds the road crosses Burrow Bridge. Continue past
the imposing gates of Burrow Hall and then at the drive of Yew Tree
Farm turn right onto the farm road.

2   Follow this as it leads towards a barn and then bends right past
a seventeenth-century farmhouse. Keep ahead through a metal gate
and continue past a barn. After this, bear left to a wall crossed by a
ladder stile. Bear left towards a field corner on the rise ahead. Here,
keep ahead to the left of a wire fence as it drops to the next field
corner close to a small brook. After a metal fence cross a stone bridge
to a ladder stile. Over this, bear right in a large field to a metal gate.
Continue in the next field to a ladder stile, crossing to a drive. Turn
left on the drive and now beside Leck Beck continue for 250yds.
Where the drive turns left, keep ahead on a narrow footpath, which
leads to Cowan Bridge on the busy A65.

3   Cross the bridge and walk along the A65 to the bus shelter.
Behind this, turn right onto a narrow path that soon reaches open
fields. Keep ahead, crossing four fields until you reach Overtown.

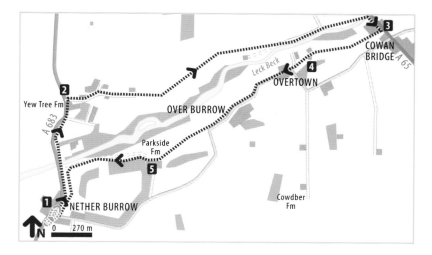

④ Here, a wooden stile leads into a grassy lane between properties. At its end turn left through a small wooden gate, cutting across a parking area to reach a drive. This leads down to a lane. Keep ahead. There now follows 700yds of road walking. Where the road bends sharply left, keep ahead at a wooden gate leading into a large field. Keep ahead towards Parkside Farm.

⑤ When you reach it, go through a wooden gate to the left of two metal ones and bear right into the main yard. Once past a large barn, turn right and after a metal gate bear left as you enter a long field. As the field narrows between woods to the left and the tree-lined Leck Beck on the right, bear right to follow the fence. In the far corner a ladder stile leads onto the A683 close to Burrow Bridge. Turn left for the inn.

Points of interest

On reaching the A65 at Cowan Bridge, the cottages to the left are of interest. These once housed the Clergy Daughters' School attended by Charlotte Brontë and her sisters Emily, Maria and Elizabeth. Conditions were so dire that typhus broke out, killing Maria and Elizabeth and no doubt compromising the health of Charlotte and Emily. There is a commemorative plaque on the wall.

Skippool

START Skippool car park,
FY5 5LF, SD357411

DISTANCE 4 miles (6.4km)

SUMMARY Easy

MAP OS Explorer 296 Lancaster,
Morecambe & Fleetwood

WHERE TO EAT AND DRINK
The River Wyre Hotel,
www.vintageinn.co.uk,
theriverwyrepoultonlefylde/,
T01253-893428

A walk of surprising contrasts in a suburban location.

① From the car park turn left, and with the river on your right
pass the Blackpool and Fleetwood Yacht Club. A little under 300yds
beyond the club turn left through trees on a footpath leading to
Thornton Hall Farm.

② Keep ahead to Woodhouse Rd, which leads onto the B5412
Turn left and then right into Tarn Rd. After following a bend to the
right, cross to Links Gate and follow it down to an area of exclusive
property to a footpath between high fences. This arrives at the busy
Amounderness Way.

③ Cross the road, turn left and then almost immediately right onto
a footpath, which leads onto Poulton Golf Club. The right of way
crosses the course with the occasional waymark heading towards the
clubhouse. Keeping to the edge of fairways after crossing a footbridge,
bear right to the tall hedgerow marking the boundary of the course.
Here, almost in line with the clubhouse, locate a stile leading onto a
wooded path. Turn left and follow the path to Breck Rd.

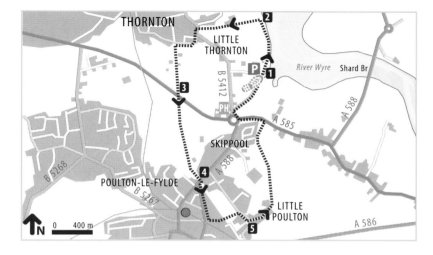

④ Turn right and then left into Station Rd. Continue to the railway bridge and then just before it take a path on the left that cuts through to Howarth Crescent. At the end of the street continue on a footpath. Where the path divides bear left to reach Moorland Rd, alongside Hodgson Academy. Turn right to go past the front of the school and then turn left into Little Poulton Lane.

⑤ Follow the lane past properties ancient and modern to its end. Here, take a footpath signposted 'Skippool ¾ mile'. This leads across fields to the banks of Main Dyke. When you reach it, turn left. Keep on the path to reach Mains Rd. Turn left.

The idea now is to cross a busy roundabout to turn right onto the B5412 and then right again into Wyre Lane. This leads round to Skippool car park.

Points of interest

Looking at the moorings beyond the yacht club, it is difficult to imagine the thriving sea port that Skippool once was. Indeed, at the start of the eighteenth century it conducted more trade than Liverpool, with ships coming in from Russia and Barbados.

START Croston village centre,
close to the Grapes Hotel,
PR26 9RA, SD490185

DISTANCE 4½ miles (7.2km)

SUMMARY Flat; mainly farm
tracks and some road walking

MAP OS Explorer 285
Southport & Chorley

WHERE TO EAT AND DRINK
There are a number of pubs in
Croston; most serve food

This walk starts in the village, then follows the Yarrow to its confluence with the
River Douglas, before returning by way of the moss.

1️⃣ Cross the ancient packhorse bridge across the Yarrow and turn
right into the Hillocks. Follow the lane between rustic brick barns
and turn right at the junction. At the next junction cross the road and
take a short ginnel between houses. Turn right and follow the street to
where it joins the Southport Rd by some Georgian almshouses.

2️⃣ Turn left onto the A581. For the time being it is best keeping to
the left side where there is a narrow pavement. Make the most of the
bridge as it crosses the railway – it is the highest point on the walk.
Continue to a slight bend, then cross the road to a stile on top of the
embankment. The River Yarrow soon meets the River Lostock and
then, after passing under pylons, joins the River Douglas. Follow the
embankment around on its wide sweep to the left. Further along on
the opposite bank you will see a pumping station that helps to drain
the rich farmland. A short way beyond the pump house you come to
Great Hanging Bridge.

3️⃣ Cross the road and follow a track as it bears left in front of a
works depot. In 250yds, at a junction, turn right. This is Shepherd's
Lane. Keep on it for approximately 500yds – 7 or 8mins – and then
follow the main track as it bends to the left towards the electricity
pylons. At the level crossing take the advice of the warning signs.

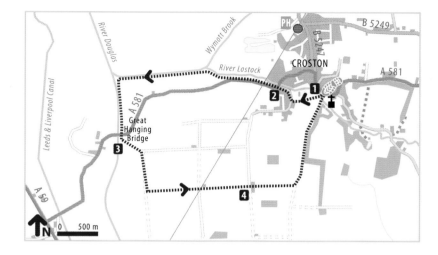

There are not many trains along the Preston–Ormskirk line but it would only take one to turn you into coarse mince!

④ Keep ahead at the next junction of tracks past Moss House Farm. The track now begins to upgrade itself and by the time it reaches Sumner's Farm it is fully metalled. The lane swings to the left towards the village with hedges on either side, the first hint of enclosures since the walk commenced. The lane will bring you to the edge of Croston. After passing a farm entrance on the right, turn right at the next corner towards the cemetery. Take the footpath on the left that crosses the Yarrow and leads through the old village school to the churchyard. Bear left into Church St.

Points of interest

Local inquiry has not revealed the derivation of the name of Great Hanging Bridge, other than to distinguish it from Little Hanging Bridge. One plausible suggestion is that it was built after the River Douglas was channelled away from its original course so that the original bridge, now Little Hanging Bridge, was left hanging there to no purpose.

START The wharf at Foulridge
on the Leeds–Liverpool Canal,
BB8 7PP, SD888426

DISTANCE 4½ miles (7.2km)

SUMMARY Moderate

MAP OS Explorer OL21
South Pennines

WHERE TO EAT AND DRINK
Café Cargo,
http://cafecargo.co.uk,
T01282-865069; it offers the
only parking on the wharf so it's
a good idea to have a cuppa at
the start or end of the walk

An exploration of a delightful part of the county.

① From the wharf return to Warehouse Lane and keep ahead as
the road crosses Towngate. Continue for 100yds and turn right into
Sycamore Rise. Follow the road round to the left, passing a children's
playground on your left, and onto a short unmarked path ahead.
Cross Alma Av and go down a path next to No. 37 to the side of Lake
Burwain. Turn right along a path edging the reservoir. After the
boathouse drop to a road and go past a 'Private Road' sign. Shortly
after Sand Hall turn left over a stile and follow the path to Slipper Hill
Reservoir. At the far end of the reservoir bear right to reach a lane.
Turn right on the lane.

② Walk up the lane for 300yds, then on reaching a converted
farmhouse turn right across its front and cross a stile beyond it. Go
along a wall, crossing two stiles, and go right across a field towards a
gate. Follow a path round the corner of Greenshaw Farm's garden and
continue past the front of the farm to a stile. Continue along a track
and after the next farm take a track on the left to a gate with a stile.
Go diagonally right across the field ahead to cross a stream and then
a stile into a walled track. Turn left and continue for 300yds to reach
a facing stile. Cross and follow a wall to reach a circular walk sign at
a stile. Cross and follow these signs, passing the drive of an imposing

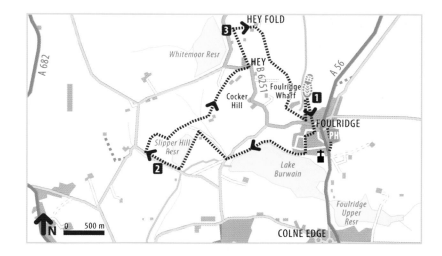

property on the right to reach a road. Turn right. Continue to a post box. Now turn left and left again between houses and bungalows, going through a farm. Keep on the lane to reach a small gate leading onto a path. Keep on this past the converted chapel to reach a lane.

③   Turn right. After Hey Fold farmhouse turn right onto a footpath. Cross the field ahead, go over a stile and along a wall on your right. Cross a stile in a field corner, continue over two streams and cross a stile between holly bushes. Cross the bottom of the field, a stile, a lane, a field and another stile onto a road. Turn left to reach a stile. Cross the next field and follow the wall around. Go over a stile onto a road. Keep on this as it leads back to Foulridge.

Points of interest

At the start of the walk take time to view the entrance to Foulridge Tunnel, one of the wonders of the canal age. Completed in 1796, it is almost a mile long.

Great Mitton

START Close to the Three Fishes Inn, opposite Church Lane, Great Mitton, BB7 9PQ, SD715389

DISTANCE 4½ miles (7.2km)

SUMMARY Mainly flat and easy

MAP OS Explorer OL41 Forest of Bowland

WHERE TO EAT AND DRINK
The Three Fishes, Great Mitton, www.thethreefishes.com, T01254-826888;
The Hillcrest Tearooms, Great Mitton, T01254-826 573;
The Edisford Bridge, T01200-422637

This short walk will introduce you to a lovely reach of the River Ribble, with a classic view of Pendle Hill along part of the Ribble Way, a long-distance path following the river from the sea to its source on a 70-mile trail.

① The first part of the walk follows the Ribble Way to Edisford Bridge. With the Three Fishes on your right, walk slightly downhill passing the church opposite and the Old Hall. The road leads down to Mitton Bridge, which crosses the River Ribble. Cross it, passing the Aspinall Arms pub, and then turn left through a wooden kissing gate.

② Follow the field boundary as it leads gently uphill to a stile in a wooden fence. Over this, bear left and then after a kissing gate enter a large riverside pasture. Beyond a small service building, join a riverside track leading up to a utility bridge spanning the river. Here, continue through a wooden gate on a track that soon brings you to Shuttleworth Farm. Keep on through the farm. After the river bends away, keep ahead for another 500yds to reach a junction immediately beyond woods on the left. Turn left here and then right onto a track a short distance from the junction. Almost immediately go through the kissing gate that leads to an enclosed path. This soon reunites you with the river. The path enters the Riverside Park just before Edisford Bridge. Keep ahead through the playground and car park to join Edisford Rd (B6243). Turn left.

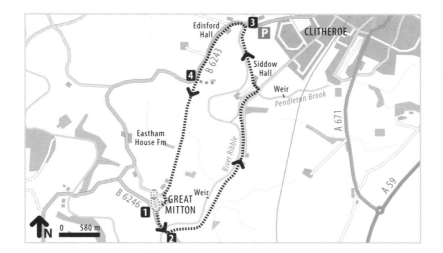

③ Now keep firmly to the right side of the road as it climbs up past the Edisford Bridge Inn. Keep on the main road past the junction for Balshall and continue for another 800yds. Where the road bends sharply right, cross to the drive of a farm.

④ Turn right onto a farm road. After crossing a stile next to a metal gate, continue on the tarmac to the next gate. At this, bear slightly right to cross a stile leading into a large field. Follow the hedge to your left as it leads you across fields by a series of wooden stiles. After the way crosses a culvert, the next stile leads into a vast field; keeping parallel to the hedge on the left, cross this. A short distance beyond a small enclosed pond, turn left over a stile onto a narrow path known as Malkin Lane. Keep on it for 300yds until it brings you onto a quiet lane opposite a house. This is in fact Church Lane. Turn left and you'll soon arrive in Great Mitton.

The Guild Wheel & Brockholes

START The Pavilion, Avenham
Park, Preston, PR1 8JT, SD539286

DISTANCE 4½ miles (7.2km)

SUMMARY Easy

MAP OS Explorer 286
Blackpool & Preston

WHERE TO EAT AND DRINK
The Pavilion, Avenham Park,
T01772-90773; there is a large
restaurant at the Brockholes
Wildlife Trust Reserve Visitor
Centre, T01772-872000

A walk along the Guild Wheel from Preston centre to the Wildlife Trust Reserve at
Brockholes.

1   This description covers the first (or last!) 4 miles of the Guild
Wheel to Brockholes. From the Pavilion join the riverside path and,
with the Ribble on your right, head upstream. After the Old Tram
Bridge the route quickly reaches the Boulevard and from there
continues to the London Road Bridge. There is a dedicated pedestrian
crossing to help negotiate the busy A6.

2   Over the road, pass to the side of the Shawes Arms and then soon
after walkers can cross a stile on the right and continue on the Ribble
Way across fields to reunite with the cycle route 1½ miles further on
near Mete House.

3   After passing below the A59 at Brockholes Bridge and soon after
the M6, the route reaches the entrance to Brockholes Wildlife Trust
Reserve, which is on the left immediately after the motorway ramp.

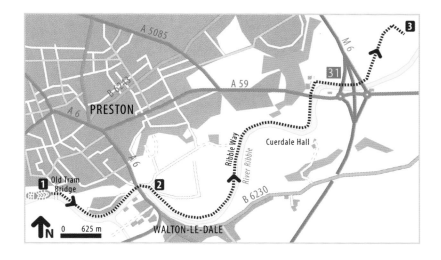

Points of interest

The Guild Wheel is the 21-mile multi-use greenway that has been developed as an enduring legacy from the 2012 Preston Guild celebrations (www.preston.gov.uk). In essence it is a cycleway that circles the city, in the main following the green belt. Like a bicycle wheel it has been designed with 'spokes', providing links with the city centre along established routes of the National Cycle Network.

Brockholes Wildlife Trust Reserve is a bold, imaginative and far-sighted project. On the site of a former gravel quarry a range of habitats has been created to encourage and protect wildlife. This is a showcase venture and it is most fitting that the visitor centre floating on the edge of Meadow Lake won design awards in 2011. The centre sits on a concrete raft constructed with hollow chambers for buoyancy.

Hurstwood

START United Utilities car park
(pay & display) near Hurstwood
Reservoir, BB10 3LF, SD881312

DISTANCE 4½ miles (7.2km)

SUMMARY Moderate. This route
demands accurate navigation

MAP OS Explorer OL21
South Pennines

Hurstwood is one of those secret places well known to locals but not much
known outside the area. It is tucked away in the hills close to Burnley on the
edge of the South Pennines.

1⃣ From the car park walk back towards the village. Turn right in
front of the chapel and then join the track below the conifer plantation
at the dam end of Hurstwood Reservoir (as yet unseen). Now on the
Burnley Way, enter the woods and keep on the path that edges along
them. (Note: 150yds along, a path on the right takes you down directly
to the dam end of the reservoir. When you reach it, turn left and
continue to the footbridge described in 2⃣ .)

2⃣ At the far corner of the plantation turn right to drop to a broad
track close to the shores of the reservoir. On joining it, turn left.
Follow this as it crosses a footbridge at the top of the reservoir. At the
next junction of tracks the Burnley Way joins the Pennine Bridleway.
Turn left. The track climbs up to the Gorple Rd 700yds further along.
When you reach it, turn right. The Gorple Rd is one of the finest
moorland tracks in the north of England. For the next 1,200yds it
gradually climbs up to the highest point on the route (1,300ft), not far
from the border with Yorkshire.

3⃣ After 1,200yds, or about 15mins of steady climbing, where the
track crosses a culverted stream turn right on a faint path. (There is
not much by way of feature to help you here other than the GR, which
is SD909322, and the fact that if you arrive at a gate you have overshot
the path by 500yds.) Follow the path across rough moorland, keeping

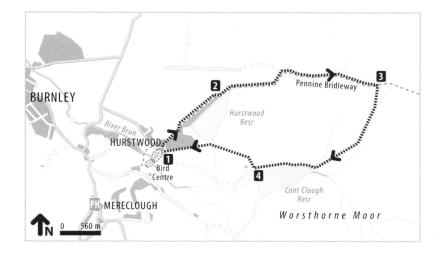

the stream to the left on a gradual descent to Cant Clough Reservoir. When you reach the eastern tip of the reservoir, turn right on a broad track that follows the shore to the dam end.

4 Here, once again link up with the Pennine Bridleway. Follow it right on a utilities service road, taking you up over a brow to Hurstwood Reservoir. As the track makes a wide sweep to the right before the reservoir, go through a kissing gate on the left and enter woodland to reach a broad track. Turn left and follow this back to the car park.

Points of interest

The Pennine Bridleway was inspired by the campaign of Lady Mary Towneley of Lancashire, who saw the need for a long-distance track suitable for horse-riders and cyclists. She died about the time the trail was established. In memory of her work, a 76-mile circuit was created in the South Pennines and called the Mary Towneley Loop.

START Small car park, Killiard
Lane, by Billinge Hill, Pleasington,
BB2 6QA, SD653281

DISTANCE 4½ miles (7.2km)

SUMMARY Easy

MAP OS Explorer 287
West Pennine Moors

WHERE TO EAT AND DRINK
The Clog and Billycock,
www.theclogandbillycock.com,
T01254-201163

USEFUL WEBSITES
www.blackburn.gov.uk for details
about the Witton Weavers Way;
www.wainwright.org.uk, the
website of the Wainwright Society

A walk that concludes with a visit to a memorial to the most famous walker of all
– Alfred Wainwright, who was born in nearby Blackburn.

1 Walk back up the lane to Billinge End Rd and turn left. In a little
under 300yds you will arrive at the Clog and Billycock. Opposite
the car park take the footpath, which leads narrowly past a garage.
Dropping gently downhill, at first with a hedge on the right, bear right
at a telephone pole to reach a field corner opposite Westholme School.
Continue down the lane opposite to the left of the school. Keep ahead
at Shorrock Farm and, when you reach a property, cross its lawn
on the left side. Continue gently downhill with a fence on your left.
After 150yds cross a stile on the left next to a metal gate and continue
downhill with the fence now on your right to a footbridge.

2 Cross the brook, climb the embankment and turn left. After a
plank bridge bear diagonally right to a stile next to the gate. Over this,
follow the hedge on your right to reach Lodge Wood. The path crosses
a drive and then leads up to a stile by a metal gate. Cross the stile and
turn left, following the edge of Woodfold Park Estate. After passing an
impressive house, the path continues to Further Lane. Here, turn left.

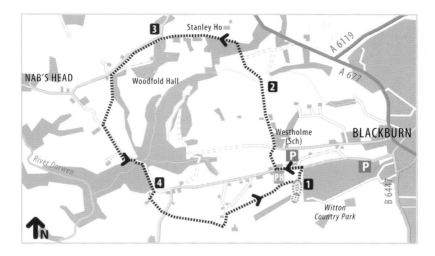

③ Keep on the lane for 700yds. After passing Ravenswing Farm on the right, turn left onto a footpath leading down to a stile and enter a large field. Keep ahead to a stile close to a metal gate. Beyond this, the path swings right, aiming towards a tall radio mast. When you reach the lane, turn left. Some 350yds after joining the lane, bear left through a wooden side gate onto a broad track. Soon this enters woodland, descending to a bridge over Arley Brook. On the far side the track climbs steeply to emerge close to Alum Scar House. Turn right. Just before you reach Close Farm, turn left over a stile.

④ You are now on the Witton Weavers Way for the rest of the walk. The footpath leads across two fields to reach Pleasington Rd. Cross the lane onto a farm drive. Keep ahead when the drive bends to the right. The path is well waymarked as you cross fields, at first with a hedge to the left and then over open ground. After the trail enters woods close to Butlers Delf it turns left and then before a property turns right on a path leading up to a stile crossing into pastureland. Cross this and keep heading up to the top of the hill. This modest height provides one of the best viewpoints in the whole of Lancashire. From the top keep ahead towards a stile close to a tree. Beyond this, the path leads back to the car park.

START The Square, just off Clifton Dr, St-Annes-on-Sea (A584), FY8 1RG, SD319287

DISTANCE 4½ miles (7.2km)

SUMMARY Easy

MAPS OS Explorer 286 Blackpool & Preston, though the OS street atlas for Lancashire will be just as useful

WHERE TO EAT AND DRINK There are numerous pubs, restaurants and cafés on or close to St Anne's Square

Mark Twain famously observed that golf 'is a good walk spoiled'. So this walk takes you around the historic golf course of Royal Lytham & St Annes and concludes with a bracing seaside promenade.

1 Keep ahead in the Square, following West Crescent, which crosses the railway – just about the only ascent of the walk. Opposite Our Lady Star of the Sea Catholic church turn right into St David's Rd South. After 400yds turn left and then right into St Patrick's Rd South. This leads onto Links Gate, which unsurprisingly brings you to the rear of the famous clubhouse of Royal Lytham & St Annes Golf Club.

2 The next part of the walk follows the perimeter of the golf course. Follow Links Gate left, and then in the direction of the cycle route turn right onto a street that leads onto Beauclerk Rd. Good views of the course open up. Keep ahead to enter a pedestrian/cycle track between college fields on the left and the course on the right. This brings you to a cul-de-sac (Central Dr).

3 At the next junction turn right into Worsley Rd, and then on a bend of the road keep ahead on a footpath leading straight across the course. Pay attention to the warning signs. After crossing the course, continue over the railway (which runs parallel to the front nine holes) and turn left into Arundel Rd. Follow this and as you near the station turn right and then left to arrive on Woodlands Rd. Turn right.

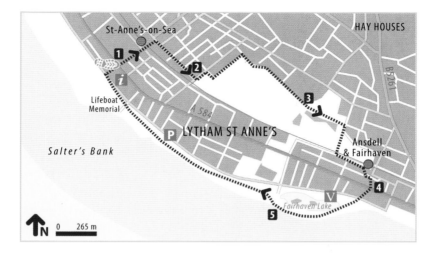

④ Pass the Methodist church on the corner of Clifton Dr and cross to Marine Dr. From here, quickly reach the promenade. Cross to Stanner Bay car park, walking alongside Fairhaven Boating Lake to reach the walkway along the shore. Turn right.

⑤ There now follows a fine coastal walk, which beyond concrete and tarmac enters an area of dunes. With the Irish Sea on your left, keep ahead until you reach the promenade at St Annes. From the pier turn right, cross to St Annes Rd and return to the Square.

Points of interest

On the promenade close to the pier is a memorial to the Mexico lifeboat disaster. In 1886 three lifeboats from Southport, Lytham and St Annes were launched to assist the stricken Mexico, a 400-ton sailing barque caught in a storm off Southport. Its crew was rescued but two lifeboats capsized with the loss of twenty-seven lives. It is the worst loss of a RNLI crew to date.

Start Car park at Potts Corner, LA3 3LL (nearby), SD417512

Distance 4½ miles (7.2km)

Summary Mainly flat and easy but care may be needed along the seashore near Sunderland Point

Map OS Explorer 296 Lancaster, Morecambe & Fleetwood

This walk passes 'Sambo's Grave', a poignant reminder of the county's connections with the slave trade.

① With the wide expanse of Morecambe Bay on your right, walk along the track beyond its fork to Alderley Bank. When the track turns up the embankment after 600yds, keep straight along a narrow path with the fence still on your left. After passing Sunderland Brows Farm you will come to a footpath sign for Sunderland. Continue along the shore and a short way ahead in a small enclosure you will reach Sambo's Grave.

② After paying due respect continue along the shore to reach Sunderland Point. Here the Lune enters Morecambe Bay. Walk round the Point in a northerly direction towards Sunderland. When the tide is in you will have to negotiate a rock strewn shore, or even the rock sea defence bank, to reach the hamlet. Walk along its front, now on the road, which at low tide connects Sunderland with the outside world.

③ Bear left on a track past the last house in the settlement. Ahead there is an embankment. Follow the track as it bends to the right to reach a ladder stile with a signpost indicating a footpath to Low Rd. Keep ahead, aiming for a footbridge by a telegraph pole, and continue across five fields, aided by stiles and footbridges. As you near Trailholme, a prominent farm complex on a rise, you will arrive at a ladder stile. Cross it to climb an embankment, then turn right towards the farm. Look for a ladder stile on the left, which will put you on a

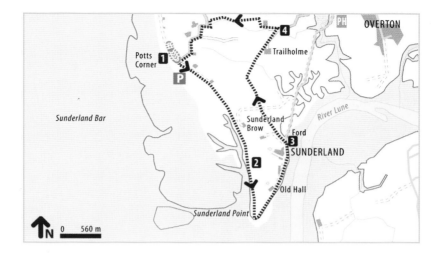

good farm track. Take the track past the farm to its junction with the lane, and then turn left to another farm complex – Trumley Farm/ Marsh Lea.

4 In front of the farms take the right fork track to Marsh Lea. Passing the buildings on the left, cross a stile and then keep ahead on a track to reach a junction of footpaths. Here, turn left through a gate. Keep ahead to cross another stile. At the bottom right of the next field cross another stile and then follow the left edge of the field past a waymark post around to a ladder stile by a track junction, close to a motor repair yard. Continue straight on along the yard, following the track to its junction with Carr Lane. Turn left to return to the car park by road in 10mins.

Points of interest

Details are sparse as to who 'Sambo' was. The main inscription dated 1796 indicates that he died sixty years previously when the slave trade was at its height. Whether he was a slave or a freeman, he was certainly a long way from home. It is hard to imagine a lonelier or more desolate place for this solitary grave. Yet despite this, it is covered with tender remembrances on inscribed pebbles and stones.

START The Green, Wrea Green, PR4
2PH, SD397315 (roadside parking)

DISTANCE 4½ miles (7.2km)

SUMMARY Easy

MAP OS Explorer 286
Blackpool & Preston

WHERE TO EAT AND DRINK
Dizzy Ducks Tea Rooms,
T01772-468675;
The Grapes,
www.chefandbrewer.com/pub/
grapes-hotel,
T01772-682927

This walk starts and ends in one of Lancashire's most attractive villages and will
take you out onto the farmland of the Fylde.

① From the north-east corner of the Green continue along the
B5259, now Moss Side Lane, passing the duck pond and then the
war memorial. You soon get the sense of leaving the village. About
300yds from the Green, where the road bends pronouncedly to the
right, take a footpath on the left next to the drive of a house. At first
you are on a farm track, soon to become grassy. It leads down to a
stile. Once across it, keep ahead with a hedge on your left, passing
below electricity pylons. After a footbridge continue over gently rising
ground in the same direction, with the hedge now on your right. The
footpath will bring you to a narrow lane (Bryning Hall Lane).

② Turn left. The lane dog-legs past imposing New House Farm to
reach Bryning Hall Farm and then, a little way beyond, the hamlet
of Bryning, which rather unsurprisingly is on Bryning Lane. Cross
Bryning Lane, pass the equestrian centre and follow the farm track
that will lead out to Green Valley Farm and then Prospect Farm.
'Prospect' seems an apt name because on the slight inclines of the
Fylde you will have remarkably distant views – Beacon Fell and the
Chipping Fells to the east; the West Pennine Moors to the south-east.
From Prospect Farm follow a grassy track to its end and then after
a kissing gate follow the field boundary on your right. It would be
quicker to walk diagonally left across this field to a stile. However,

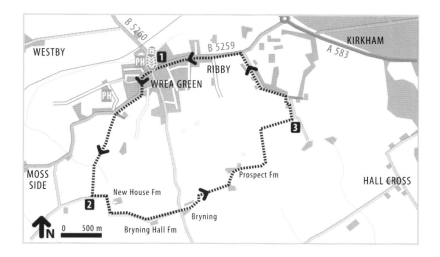

the right of way edges around the field and passes beneath pylons; in effect you have turned a sharp left from the previous direction of travel. Keep alert for there is another sharp turn 250yds or so after the pylons. This time turn right over a narrow stile. Crossing two fields you will arrive at a farm lane.

3 Turn left. The farm road quickly joins Brown's Lane and continues alongside Ribby Hall holiday complex on the right. When you reach Ribby Rd (B5259), turn left for the village. A 15min walk will bring you to the Green.

Points of interest

Wrea Green has exactly what it says on the tin – a green. And not just any old scrap of turf the landowners forgot to enclose in the eighteenth century, but a proper green – one to practise archery or play cricket on, complete with duck pond and gorgeous cottages looking out onto it.

White Coppice ▶

START Small car park, White Coppice, PR6 9DE, SD614191 (further parking available near the cricket ground)

DISTANCE Short route 4½ miles (7.2km); long route 6½ miles (10.5km)

SUMMARY Farmland and woodland tracks. Mainly easy walking with some short ascents

MAP OS Explorer 287 West Pennine Moors

Two routes that explore the edge of the West Pennine Moors.

1️⃣ Just before a row of cottages on the left, cross a footbridge next to a ford. Steadily climb the track to where it bends to the right. Keep ahead, crossing a stile by a metal gate. Continue with the hedge on your left, then on your right. The path drops to a wooded corner. After crossing a wooden stile, cross a small brook to reach a second stile. Once across, enter a field and continue with a fence on your right. Drop to a metal gate in the corner. Go through, cross a bridge over the disused railway and turn left on a farm track. Where this meets a lane after 200yds, turn right. This lane will bring you to a cluster of houses. Keep straight and then follow the lane as it bends to the right in trees to reach a large house. Past the entrance continue to a junction of footpaths. Keep ahead, crossing a field with a fence on your right. The footpath enters woods by way of a gate. Turn left onto a wide track that leads up to Brinscall Hall. After the track turns left in front of the hall, turn right for Brinscall.

2️⃣ Turn right into School Lane and descend through the village. To follow the short route, take the road down to Butterworth Brow and bear right into Well Lane and after 300yds turn right into Wheelton Plantation (from here, jump to 4️⃣). The longer route turns left after 200yds onto a footpath signed for Withnell and Abbey village. Keep on this to reach Withnell local nature reserve and beyond it Abbey village. Turn right onto the A675.

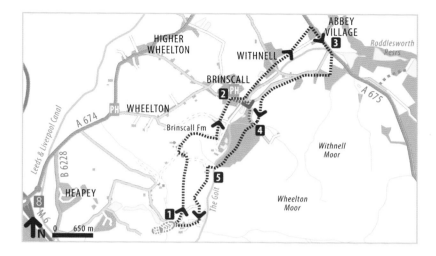

③ From the Hare and Hounds at the south end of the village, walk a further 200yds towards Bolton, then turn right onto a footpath. This leads up to a timber yard. Follow the path as it bears to the left and then turns right to enter the yard. Cross the yard and then turn right to reach the lane. Turn left on the lane. Where the lane divides 400yds ahead, keep left to join Twist Moor Lane. Continue for 700yds, past a quarry on the left and before the lane drops to Brinscall, then turn left onto a footpath. This leads across rough pasture. Where the path forks, keep right to arrive at a stile leading into a lane. Turn left and then, after a short distance, right onto a broad track leading through Wheelton Plantation.

④ Keep on this track as it curves through the trees and begins to gently descend. After 700yds the track reaches a footbridge.

⑤ Cross the footbridge and turn immediately left. You are now walking alongside the Goit, an artificial waterway feeding the reservoirs downstream. Keep on the concessionary path for 800yds to a small reservoir. With the reservoir on your left, cross a field to reach a footbridge. Over this, follow the path onto the cricket ground. Turn right, skirting the field. When you reach the cinder lane, descend to the car park.

Ashurst's Beacon

START Beacon Country Park car park on Mill Lane, Upholland (known as Carr Lane car park), WN8 7RU, SD508065

DISTANCE 5 miles (8km)

SUMMARY Easy, with a very short, sharp ascent to Ashurst's Beacon. The route ends with a 25min walk along a lane that can be busy at weekends

MAP OS Explorer 285 Southport & Chorley

WHERE TO EAT AND DRINK
The Prince William Inn, www.princewilliaminndalton. robinsonsbrewery.com, T01695-623989;
The Beacon Inn, www.marstonspubcompany.co.uk, T01695-622771

USEFUL WEBSITE
www.westlancs.gov.uk for information about Beacon Country Park

This walk – a short distance from Skelmersdale – offers surprising countryside close to a densely populated part of the county.

① From the trig point close to the car park there is a superb view towards Liverpool and the Clwydian Hills beyond. From the car park walk onto Mill Lane, turning left, and after about 80yds on the opposite side of the road take the footpath sign indicated alongside the first house. The footpath takes you through meadows, where you keep the field boundary on your left. After about 15mins of gentle descent you will see a bungalow on the left; go through the stile on the left just after the bungalow, which leads you onto a lane. Turn right.

② A short distance ahead, take the public footpath unusually indicated on the gate into an attractive property. The path leads to the left of the house and reaches open fields. After 300yds the path joins a track. Follow the track as it skirts woodland, then where the track turns pronouncedly left keep on it to just before the iron pole barrier (leading to shooting land). Here, take the footpath on the right indicated by the waymarker. The footpath leads through trees into arable land beyond. When the footpath meets a track, turn left. After 100yds turn right downwards through trees, finding a waymarked path that will bring you to the rear of a farm with a row of handsome poplars. The path

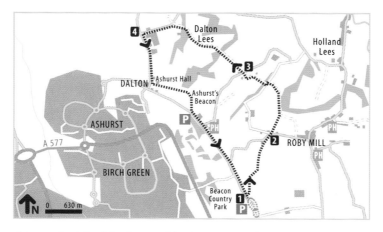

skirts to the left of the farm and leads out onto a lane.

(3) Cross the lane onto a track that initially has the hedge on its right. After crossing a stretch of open arable land, the route passes through a ribbon of woodland to reach another track. Turn left, passing a footbridge on your left, and then continue 100yds to cross a footbridge and go through a kissing gate. Begin a gentle ascent in the next pasture. The track becomes more obvious as you walk on, turning into a proper track that leads onto a brick track leading to Hillock Lane. Turn left and after 400yds turn left again into Higher Lane.

(4) After about 700yds turn left at the primary school before the church towards Ashurst Hall. This path soon leads you up a sharp incline to Ashurst's Beacon, one of the finest viewpoints in the county. From the folly descend on a broad grassy track, dropping into Beacon Lane. Turn left and walk along the road, first passing the Beacon Inn, closely followed by The Prince William public house, and after 25mins arriving back at the car park.

Points of interest

The original beacon formed a chain of signal fires at the time of the Spanish Armada (1588). During the Napoleonic Wars the landowner Sir William Ashurst set up this more permanent structure.

Bolton-by-Bowland

START Information Centre and
car park, Bolton-by-Bowland,
BB7 4NW, SD784494

DISTANCE 5 miles (8km)

SUMMARY Mainly easy
with one short ascent

MAP OS Explorer OL41
Forest of Bowland

Here's a walk that will give you sublime views across the Ribble Valley towards
Pendle Hill, without a great deal of ascent.

① From the car park turn left over Skirden Bridge and then
immediately right onto a footpath beside Kirk Beck. After 15 mins
cross a stile close to a garden centre. Its drive leads out onto a lane.
Turn left. Walk along the lane for 400yds and then turn right onto the
drive of a substantial farmhouse. Keep ahead through the yard and,
after a kissing gate, drop down to a footbridge. After crossing this,
bear right and go through a kissing gate leading onto a track. Turn
right. Keep on the track for 300yds as it passes through a metal gate
and approaches Hungrill.

② The route now switches back by turning left through a metal
gate at a wall end – before reaching the gateway ahead on the track.
An indistinct path follows a brook on the right before crossing it.
Keep ahead to a stile 500yds after entering the field. Walk ahead with
the hedge on the left, and as you near the lane go left through a gate
into the adjoining field and walk ahead to a stone squeeze stile in the
corner. Turn left. As you walk into the hamlet of Holden, turn right
and then left again onto a farm track.

③ Keep ahead towards the farmhouse. Take a footpath that passes to
the right of the buildings, leading to a wooden gate. Keep ahead across
the next field and, after crossing a track, bear left aiming towards a
large tree on the skyline. Beyond the tree a path leads into the next
field. Cross this to a squeeze stile followed by a stile. Keep ahead to a
stone barn. From the barn cross the next field to a metal fence below

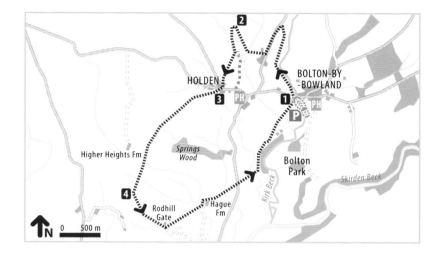

Higher Heights farm. Then cross two large fields, bearing slightly right. After a stile into the second field, aim for another on the skyline to the right. Crossing this and turning left will place you on a sunken bridleway named Rodhill Lane.

④ Follow the bridleway to join a farm road and then, as you pass Rodhill Gate, bear left across fields heading to Hague Farm. As you near the farm, bear right through a metal gate and cross the field to another. At this point you arrive on the farm track where the house has an old well by the wall side. Take a left to walk through the farmyard, following waymark signs that will lead to a pair of metal gates at the far end of the farm. After these, bear right to cross the next field to a footbridge and then continue to reach a lane.

Cross the road onto a track, then a footpath, and cross a footbridge. Keep ahead, taking the path and keeping to the right alongside the woodland boundary. Around the next field, take a stile then keep ahead, passing the remains of an ancient cross. Drop to the corner of the field and a tarmac drive leads back to the village.

START Village centre, close to the
church, Brindle, PR6 8NG, SD599242

DISTANCE 5 miles (8km)

SUMMARY Easy

MAPS OS Explorer 287 West
Pennine Moors & OS Explorer
286 Blackpool & Preston

WHERE TO EAT AND DRINK
The Cavendish Arms,
www.cavendisharms.co.uk,
T01254-852912

Although wedged in between the M65 and M61, this is a lovely walk with fine
views.

① From the church walk back along Sandy Lane 200yds and then
take a footpath on the right. This crosses a large field to reach a fence,
which it then follows on the left to arrive before Marsh Lane Farm.
Turn right onto the lane and walk along it for a little under 400yds,
and then turn left onto a farm track just before Lower Hilton's. At the
farm keep ahead through the yard. The right of way crosses the next
field, then after a stile drops through woodland to reach a footbridge.
On crossing the bridge the footpath divides – both lead to the Leeds–
Liverpool canal. Once on the towpath turn right and soon after cross
Bridge No. 88 and enter Withnell Fold.

② Follow the lane up through the settlement. About 300yds from
the canal look for a track on the right leading towards the village
recreation ground. After passing an attractive reservoir the track
continues, with the raised cricket field on the left. Beyond a metal gate
it crosses a field and then turns to the left to reach Chorley Rd (A674),
Higher Wheelton. Turn right. Keep on it for 750yds.

③ With a more open aspect on the right, turn right onto a firm
track and commence a descent back to the canal. Keep ahead as the
track bends left towards Lower Simpson Fold. Soon the canal will
come into view. Cross the canal and drop down the embankment to a
wooden footbridge. Once across it, keep ahead as the path begins to

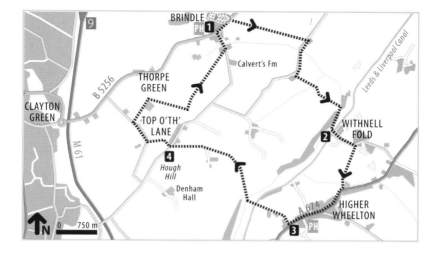

rise. Keep ahead after a stile next to a metal gate to arrive at a stile on the corner of the next field. Cross this and continue with the fence on your right to a stile in the hedge of the adjoining field. Do not cross this stile – instead turn left and, with the hedge on your right, keep going until you reach a broad farm track. This leads up to Top o' th' Lane on the skyline in front of you.

④ Cross Denham Lane onto a track taking you close to a trig point at Hough Hill. Follow the track until it comes to Holt Lane. Turn right. At Holt Lane Farm turn right and follow the track past a radio mast. Pass through the yard of Holt Farm, then bear right. The footpath leads back towards Denham Lane. After a stile in a hedge just before reaching the lane, turn left. With a field boundary initially on your left, keep ahead on an obvious path. The village will quickly come into view. The path will bring you out close by the primary school.

Points of interest

Founded in the mid-nineteenth century, the little community of Withnell Fold, originally built for the workers at the paper mill, has much to interest the curious visitor. There is an information board close to the memorial garden.

Clayton-le-Moors

START Close to Sparth House Hotel and Restaurant, Clayton-le-Moors, BB5 5RP, SD748314 (roadside parking)

DISTANCE 5 miles (8km)

SUMMARY Easy

MAP OS Explorer 287 West Pennine Moors

WHERE TO EAT AND DRINK
Sparth House Hotel,
www.sparthhousehotel.co.uk,
T01254-872263;
The Hare and Hounds,
www.thwaitespubs.co.uk,
T01254-397608 (400yds to the left as you exit the canal on Whalley Rd)

USEFUL WEBSITE
www.hyndburnbc.gov.uk

Squeezed between large industrial estates and close to the M65 at the end, this is not at first glance an appealing route, but it offers fine views on a walk full of interest.

[1]   Opposite the hotel on Whalley Rd is the entrance to The Woodlands. The route crosses to Warwick Av and continues alongside the park. Keep ahead to where the road turns to the right and join a footpath alongside the woods on the left. After a kissing gate the walk assumes a more rural character. Keep ahead to a second kissing gate giving out onto a farm track. Turn left. The track quickly leads to a cottage. Just before it, turn left through another kissing gate to enter woods. Follow the broad track and where it divides after 250yds bear right, following a wall to the right, which soon reaches open ground close by playing fields on the left. The footpath reaches a drive amongst trees. Go straight across the drive to follow the path behind properties at first on the left and then between fences left and right. At the corner turn right.

[2]   Follow the enclosed path to reach a stile leading out into a field. Skirting the edge of Clayton Hall Farm on the right, follow the path to a stile leading onto a track. Turn left. Follow the track up to Red House Farm and follow it as it turns right through the cluster of buildings. In a little over 100yds from the farm, turn left onto a green lane. This leads to Lower Moor Side Farm. Keep ahead on the broad

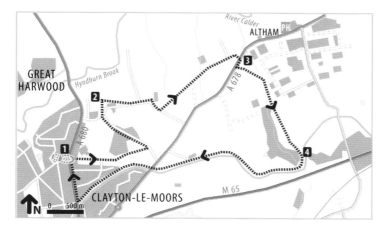

track and as it turns left to another farm continue on a footpath through a metal gate. Ignore the waymark pointing right and continue on a grassy track that leads to Syke Side Farm.

③ On reaching Burnley Rd, turn right and after 100yds turn left onto a broad unsurfaced lane. Where this divides go left in the direction of Old Engine Cottage. This leads to a large yard mainly used for vehicles. Pass to the left of the cottage and go through a stable yard to reach the field behind. The path leads up to a stile close by an industrial estate. Over this, turn right on a faint path that leads to another stile. Keep ahead to a step stile, then cross to a green lane to reach a ruined farm. Behind the ruins a stile leads onto a path that soon brings you to the Leeds–Liverpool Canal.

④ Turn right. In less than 2 miles this will take you back to Clayton-le-Moors. Exit at Bridge 114B. Turn right. Though very close to the M65 motorway, the waterway offers superb views – especially towards the Ribble Valley and the Bowland Fells.

Points of interest

The memorial to the 1883 Moorfield Colliery Disaster, a sombre reminder of the true price of coal, can be seen by coming off the canal at the Pilkington Road Bridge No. 114c. Sixty-eight men and boys (some as young as ten) perished in the disaster.

START Alkincoats Park, Colne, BB8 9QQ, SD881406

DISTANCE 5 miles (8km)

SUMMARY Easy with gentle climbs

MAP OS Explorer OL21 South Pennines

This walk, just a stone's throw from the immensely popular Boundary Mill, leads into one of the most attractive and scenic parts of Lancashire.

① From the car park take the path past the bandstand and join National Cycle Network route 68. Keep on this as it leads left through a wooded area to exit the park. Keep ahead to reach Red Lane. Cross to a stone stile opposite, leading into pastures. Cross over a ridge and then descend across wide pastures, at first with a wall on the right, to reach a lane after 500yds. Turn left. After 50yds take a footpath on the right, which leads up to Slipper Hill Reservoir. When you reach it, turn left and follow its shore back to the lane. Turn right and immediately left to cross a bridge towards houses. Turn immediately right onto a footpath leading uphill. Keep ahead for almost 400yds, then as you near a house bear left and cross to a stile leading onto Barnoldswick Rd.

② Turn left, then cross the drive leading to Malkin Tower Farm to a stile by a wooden gate. With the fence on the right, keep ahead to reach Burnt House Farm. The route passes to the right of the farm buildings and then turns left in the field beyond them. Cross to a stile close to a wall end, cross it and turn right to reach Beverley Rd. Cross to a footpath leading behind houses. Keep ahead across fields to reach a farm track leading past an unusual arched building.

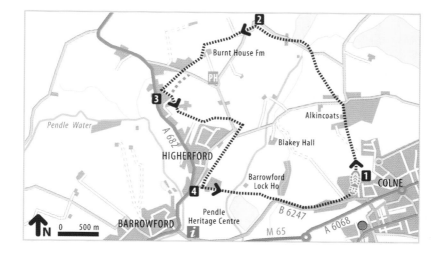

③ Just after this, turn left onto a gravelly footpath leading to a tarmac drive. Keep ahead on this towards a farm. As the drive bends to the left, go to the right and take a footpath leading into pastures. After a small wooden gate next to a metal one, keep ahead to the next gate leading into a large field. Turn left and follow the hedgerow for 100yds, then bear right to cross to a stile leading into scattered woodland. Bear right onto a path leading to a drive. Follow the drive to a road. Cross to a set of steps surmounted by a gate. Through this, cross the field to a wall, then turn right. With the wall on your left, keep ahead to reach a lane. Turn left and then right onto a footpath. At first with an ancient boundary on the left then on the right, keep ahead for 500yds. When a high wall appears on the right, follow it to a metal gate. The footpath leads to a housing estate. Turn right.

④ At the end of Grange Av turn left and keep ahead to a metal gate leading into fields. Follow the path as it crosses to the Leeds–Liverpool Canal. Cross the bridge and turn right. In 50yds turn left onto a footpath leading below Barrowford Reservoir. After a second gate the path divides. Take the left fork, which soon swings right to Barrowford Rd. When you reach the road, turn left. Keep on the road for almost half a mile, then turn into Alkincoats Rd for the park.

Garstang

START High Street car park,
Garstang, PR3 1FU, SD494455

DISTANCE Long route 6 miles
(9.7km); short route 5 miles (8km)

SUMMARY Moderate

MAP OS Explorer OL41
Forest of Bowland

Two walks from the world's first free trade town.

① From the car park join the riverside path, turning left for a bridge.
Turn right, cross and follow the track through two gates for 700yds.
The route enters a cutting. Before the next stile turn left, and climb
the embankment to reach another. Follow a path bearing right to the
rail and motorway bridges. Continue onto a lane, bear left then pass
Clarkson's Farm and at the next junction bear left again.

At Cross House turn right onto a concrete track. Keep on this for
350yds, then turn left at a stile onto a footpath leading behind Heald
Farm to a gate. Through this, turn left through the middle of three
gates and cross to a ladder stile. Over this, turn right and follow the
hedgerow up and over the hill to reach Strickens Lane in 700yds.

② (For the short route, continue along Strickens Lane for 700yds
and turn right onto the footpath opposite Walker House – see ③
for continuation.) Here, turn right and then left at the entrance of
Lancashire Racing Stables. Take a narrow path on the right, which
leads behind the buildings of LRS to a footbridge leading into a large
field. Keep ahead on the path to the corner of woods and then drop
down to Calder Vale. Turn right in front of Albert Terrace, go down
the track, and beyond Primrose Cottages bear right onto a track
leading up through woodland to a gate. Keep the fence on the left as
you cross a field to a stile and then join a track which leads to Sullom
Side Farm.

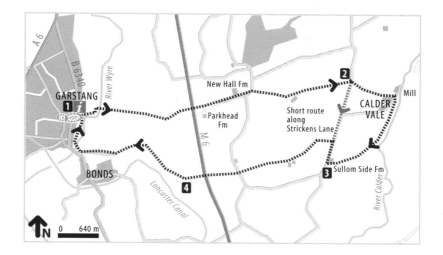

3 When you reach Strickens Lane, turn right. At Walker House turn left onto a footpath (resume short route here) and keep ahead to a gate in the right-hand corner. From here, bear left in the next field, aiming towards farm buildings. Cross a stile next to a metal gate and turn right. Turn left in front the house and in 50yds turn right onto a footpath continuing downhill. After passing farm buildings on the left, bear left to the corner. In the next field follow the fence on the right across large fields, and then at the end of a wood turn right over a stile, then bear left to a stile next to a wooden gate. Cross the lane and continue along the track to pass Bailton's Farm to reach the motorway and rail bridges.

4 Keep ahead and go through a metal gate into a large field. Aim for a solitary oak tree to locate a stile just past it. Keep ahead to pass beneath pylons through a gateway. Following the hedge on the left, cross the next stile and plank bridge, then aim to the right of farm buildings. After a small gate, keep ahead to a stile and then follow the path to the complex of buildings close to the ruins of Greenhalgh Castle. Turn left to follow the drive back to Garstang. When you reach Main St, turn right for the car park.

Hoghton Tower

START Near the Boatyard Inn,
Riley Green, PR5 0SP, SD642250

DISTANCE 5 miles (8km)

SUMMARY Easy

MAP OS Explorer 287
West Pennine Moors

WHERE TO EAT AND DRINK
The Boatyard Inn,
www.boatyardinn.co.uk,
T01254-209841;
The Royal Oak, Riley Green,
www.royaloak-rileygreen.co.uk,
T01254-201445; The Sirloin Pub &
Restaurant, Hoghton,
www.thesirloin.co.uk, T01254-852293

A walk full of interest and variety.

(1) From the car park walk across the Leeds–Liverpool canal and join its towpath on the far side of the bridge. With the canal on your right, walk towards Blackburn.

(2) After passing below two bridges, take a footpath that switches back just before a third bridge, just over a mile from where you joined the canal. The path follows green painted railings down to a large open space. Go diagonally across this and then turn left onto a service road that will bring you to the A674.

(3) Cross and turn left. At the end of a terrace of houses turn right onto a drive leading down to Hillock Farm. As the track approaches the farm buildings, take a footpath on the left. Follow a faint path to a stile in the hedge and cross it into the next field. Turn left and follow the hedge to a kissing gate in the corner. Cross the next field diagonally right to a kissing gate and enter the woods.

(4) The path now drops towards the River Darwen. On exiting the wood, follow the river across waterside meadows to arrive at another kissing gate. After passing through it, enter a narrow gorge.

(5) Keep ahead to pass beneath a railway viaduct. Beyond the viaduct the path quickly brings you to Hoghton Bottoms. After the first

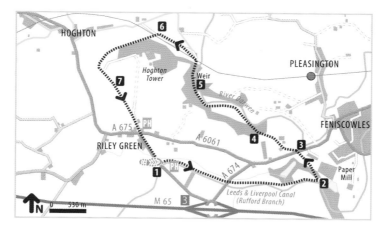

buildings bear left onto a bridleway that passes behind mill cottages to climb up towards the railway.

⑥ About 200m before reaching a road bridge turn left and cross the railway. Keep ahead in the woods to reach a high wall that marks the estate of Hoghton Tower. Turn right and keep company with the wall as the route exits the wood and enters pasture. The path follows the wall to bring you first to estate properties and then the impressive drive of the Tower itself. Cross the drive and pass through a kissing gate. Follow a track up to a gate to cross a strip of woodland.

⑦ On leaving the wood keep ahead on a path that drops to a stile. Continue down to the far left corner of the next field to reach a lane. This leads to The Royal Oak in Riley Green. Cross the road and turn onto the A675 Bolton Rd back to the car park.

Points of interest

An iconic building on the Lancashire landscape and home to the de Hoghton family from the twelfth century, the present Hoghton Tower is of more recent vintage (mid-sixteenth century). Legend has it that when King James I visited in 1617 he was so impressed with his beef that he ordered that the remains of its carcass should be brought before him, whereupon he took a sword and dubbed it 'Sir Loin' – hence the origin of the word.

Blackpool & Marton Mere

START Stanley Park, Blackpool,
FY3 9HU, SD323355

DISTANCE 5 miles (8km)

SUMMARY Flat and easy

WHERE TO EAT AND DRINK
Park's Café,
www.parksartdecocafe.co.uk,
T01253-395191, one of
Lancashire's finest art deco
buildings and a wonderful place
to have a meal or drink.

It's a safe bet that of the ten million visitors attracted to Blackpool every year few have ever gone there for a walk in its countryside. Yet the countryside is surprisingly accessible, as shown on this walk from Stanley Park.

① From the car park walk past the café, following signs for the hospital. Pass the boating lake on your right. On reaching East Park Dr, cross it at traffic lights and directly opposite take the footpath to the right of Victoria Hospital's service road (with a golf fairway on your right). The path is tree-lined on the right and has the retaining wall of the hospital on the left. At the end the path meets the tarmac of the cycle path. Soon after, turn right. At the next junction a short way ahead, turn left on a track that provides a perimeter to a golf course.

② This route is well signed. In fact there are two tracks. A cycleway/ bridleway (NCN Route No. 62) and a path that runs more or less parallel to it. Follow either in the direction of Staining and then Marton Mere, with the golf course on your right. At first the track heads north, but after 500yds it swings south.

③ After the cycle route turns left for Staining, keep ahead until you arrive at Marton Mere local nature reserve. Here, a right turn will soon take you back to Stanley Park but, by going left and circling the mere in a clockwise fashion, you will have a greater appreciation of this amenity. With the mere on your right you will reach a junction of paths a little way past the vast Marton Mere Holiday Village.

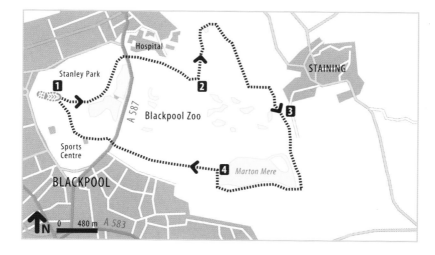

④ From here, turn left. The right of way crosses open space to East Park Dr, parallel to the drive of the De Vere Hotel. Cross near the Model Village and enter Stanley Park, walking towards the imposing monument before you. This is the Cocker Tower, named after William Henry Cocker, whose years of public service were dedicated to making Blackpool the popular holiday resort it became. From the monument turn right to the Italian Gardens and the visitors' car park.

Points of interest

First opened in 1926, Stanley Park was once considered as much a part of the Blackpool experience as a visit to the Tower Ballroom. While perhaps the 390-acre park will not see those glory days again, its future is at least promising, having attracted funding for regeneration (see www.friendsof stanleypark.org.uk). The start of the walk takes you through the park, which is worth some exploration.

Marton Mere is a local nature reserve recognized as a Site of Special Scientific Interest because of its wetlands habitats. The information board displays a map, as well as illustrations of the range of birdlife to be seen. The Rangers service building by the caravan park offers further information for visitors.

START Information Centre
and car park on Barley Lane,
Barley, BB12 9JX, SD823403

DISTANCE 5 miles (8km)

SUMMARY Though no great distance,
this is a serious moorland hike

MAP OS Explorer OL21
South Pennines

Pendle dominates its landscape, like a vast stranded whale. This walk takes you
to its summit on a classic route.

1   Turn right out of the car park entrance. At the corner, cross to
the lane opposite with the village hall on your left, leading quickly to
Barley Green. This lane soon climbs to the first of two reservoirs. At
the end of the reservoir join the Pendle Way as it comes in from the
left. For the rest of the walk you are on this trail. Beyond a stand of
pines to the right of the track, the way dips down to a wooden kissing
gate below Upper Ogden Reservoir.

2   Go through the wooden kissing gate and follow the track as
it climbs steeply to reach the higher level. The track gives way to a
narrower path between a wall and fence, then through a gate crosses
pastures to a ladder stile. Over the ladder stile follow a rough, peaty
track upwards and then along to a stream flowing from the defile that
is Boar Clough.

3   Cross the stream and follow the path for 60yds, then turn right
and climb the steep flank of the hill. As you climb, the path becomes
more obvious as it broadens out. When the route crosses the top of
Boar Clough a line of cairns comes into sight. Continue upwards
towards the trig point. The views are extensive.

4   From the trig point continue along a broad track northwards for
400yds to a wall. Do not cross the wall but bear right to quickly reach
a steep, stepped path. This is the way down. At the bottom, through a
metal kissing gate, take the path that leads right behind the farmhouse

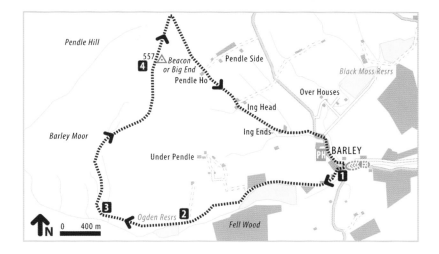

(Pendle House) and turn left, entering a large field by a gate. With a wall to your left, cross to another gate, then follow the path as it bears right across a shallow gully to enter a field close by a farmhouse. When you reach the farm road, turn right to cross the yard to a gate. This leads onto a good path beside a brook. Follow the path down to a tarmac lane at Ing Ends. Turn left, pass the attractive cottage and garden and cross a wooden footbridge on the right. The path bears left, following the course of the stream, and enters the village opposite the Methodist chapel. Turn right to reach the car park.

Points of interest

You are never far from the Witches in this part of Lancashire – they are part of the tourist industry. Indeed the logo of the Pendle Way depicts a witch on a broomstick. The story of the Lancashire Witches has the gloss of legend and public relations, but in essence what ended in a celebrated show trial at Lancaster started as a domestic row between two impoverished families in 1612. Witches were looked for and witches were found. Ten people – eight women and two men – were found guilty and executed.

Rawtenstall to Ramsbottom

START Rawtenstall ELR station,
BB4 6DD, SD809224

DISTANCE 5 miles (8km)

SUMMARY Easy and mainly flat

MAPS OS Explorer 287 West
Pennine Moors & OS Explorer
OL21 South Pennines

WHERE TO EAT AND DRINK Both
Rawtenstall and Ramsbottom have a
number of pubs, cafés and restaurants

A linear walk between stations on the East Lancashire Railway.

[1]   From the station follow the footpath on its right, skirting the
terminus buildings so that the railway is on the left. Keep on the path
as it passes the Old Cobblers Inn on your right towards a prominent
mill chimney. The way continues under an arch to enter a flagged
garden. Keep ahead. Quickly you reach a pastoral scene with the River
Irwell on the left. After passing a riverside cottage you arrive at a lane.
Turn left and cross the river on a road bridge.

[2]   Walking towards the level crossing, turn right into an area of
commercial units. At the end, turn right onto a path that is on the left
of a mesh fence and fluorescent yellow gatepost. This leads round into
a sheet metal yard. A right turn between buildings will bring you back
to the riverside path. This leads beneath the A56. After crossing a road
(B6527) at the next bridge the trail continues, passing beneath the
railway twice to arrive at the small community of Irwell Vale.

[3]   Here, turn right (not through the subway) and then cross to the
cul-de-sac opposite towards Meadow Park. After passing a converted
chapel on the right, keep ahead through a residential area. Do not cross
the bridge but keep ahead on a riverside path as it enters a wooded
stretch and soon you will find yourself walking alongside the railway
again. Turn left under the railway 200yds further on and then continue
alongside it. A short distance along there is a sculpture to view on the
hillside to the left. This next part of the walk is rather attractive as trail,

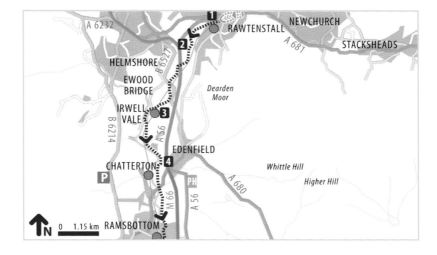

rail and water find their own route through the valley. Here you will come across more artwork that gives the trail its name.

④ As the path approaches Chatterton it reaches a track close to a footbridge. Here, turn left to walk through the settlement. Cross the A676 and continue on an unsurfaced track. You will soon come to open riverside meadows. Through a kissing gate keep to the left following a wall. After crossing a footbridge the trail takes you towards an imposing chimney, and then veers leftwards to put you on a footpath that takes you through a semi-industrial complex. When you reach a road, turn left. Keep ahead and on reaching Bridge St turn right and walk over the river to reach Ramsbottom station.

Points of interest

The East Lancashire Railway (www.eastlancsrailway.org.uk) runs from Heywood through Bury to Rawtenstall and is a marvellous example of a preserved railway run by an outstanding team of volunteers. It runs on most weekends (also through the week from May to early September). Walkers wishing to explore the Irwell Valley can use the railway to bring them back to their starting point.

WALK

52 Ribchester

START Close to the Roman Museum and St Wilfrid's church, Greenside, Ribchester, PR3 3ZJ, SD650350

DISTANCE 5 miles (8km)

SUMMARY A pleasant walk mainly across farmland

MAP OS Explorer 287 West Pennine Moors

A fascinating stroll exploring the heritage of the countryside close to Ribchester.

[1]   With the river on the right, cross the bottom of Church St on the Ribble Way. After crossing a green, turn right on Greenside, which quickly leads to the Blackburn Rd. Cross to the Ribchester Arms and then turn left onto Stydd Lane. Immediately past a church signboard, turn right onto a footpath over a stile. Cross to another in the hedgerow opposite and then bear right to a wooden footbridge. At the next stile cross the field to its far corner. Cross a stile and then turn immediately left through a wooden gate and follow a grassy track to Holmes Farm. Through its yard follow the drive to Gallows Lane. Turn right. After the next farm turn left onto a footpath that edges around the property, before crossing two stiles to reach a farm road with the River Ribble before you.

[2]   Turn left. On reaching Dewhurst House turn left in front of the farmhouse onto a bridleway, which is marked out for mountain bikes. The white posts act as a helpful guide at first, but when more open ground is reached aim for the corner of Stewarts Wood ahead. After a wooden gate follow the edge of the wood to its far corner. Here, bear left towards a wooded valley. Follow the path down to a gate and then climb the rise after aiming for the centre of a line of telephone poles. Keep ahead to reach a farm road beyond a pair of metal gates.

[3]   Turn left. Keep on the farm road as it leads gently uphill for 900yds to skirt alongside Grindlestone House Farm. As you reach its far side, turn left through its yard and cross to a stile by a metal gate. Keep ahead to a wooden stile and then, after a double stile and plank

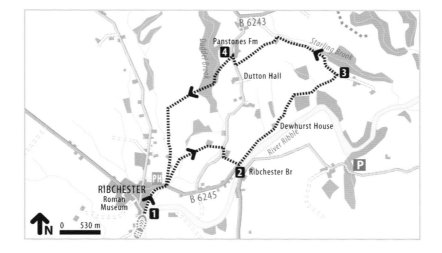

bridge, continue with a hedgerow on your left. Just before a sharp slope (site of an old quarry), cross a stile on the left into the adjoining field and then drop down to the right corner to reach Gallows Lane. Turn right. After passing a drive entrance on the left, turn left onto a footpath over a stile.

4 This crosses to a metal gate and then drops to the bottom left corner of the field and Duddel Wood. After a wooden stile continue through trees to reach a broad path by Duddel Brook. Turn left and then after a footbridge climb the rise to a stile leading into pasture land. Keep ahead, following the field boundary on the left. The way dips to a stile and then, maintaining the same direction, crosses a wide field to a stile next to a wooden gate. Cross it and turn left onto a grassy track leading down to Stydd Manor. Follow the path to the right of the farm buildings into the yard and then join the lane returning you to Blackburn Rd. From here, retrace your outward route.

Points of interest

If time allows, visit the Roman Museum (www.ribchesterroman museum.org.uk), which contains some interesting exhibits explaining the Roman occupation of this part of their empire.

Scorton

START This description starts at Scorton post office, where the Wyresdale Wheels tramper can be picked up (T01524-791329), PR3 1AU, SD501487

DISTANCE Tramper trail 5 miles (8km); walking route 4½ miles (7.2km)

SUMMARY Tramper Category 1

MAP OS Explorer OL41 Forest of Bowland

WHERE TO EAT AND DRINK The Priory, www.theprioryscorton.co.uk, T01524-791255; The Barn gift shop & coffee bar, www.plantsandgifts. co.uk, T01524-793533; The Apple Store Café in Wyresdale Park, http://wyresdalepark.co.uk/cafe-gardens

An outing for tramper users and walkers from one of Lancashire's most popular villages.

TRAMPER TRAIL

(1) From the post office turn right towards Garstang along Gubberford Lane for 300yds. Turn left into Tithebarn Lane. This dips beneath the M6 motorway and then climbs up for half a mile to Higher Lane.

(3) Turn right. After 100yds, where the lane bends to the right, keep ahead through a wooden gate and follow the track down to open pasture. Cross the valley (the only truly off-road section of the circuit) to a metal gate. Turn left into the lovely Grizedale Valley. Keep on the track as it gently climbs up to a gate close to Grizedale Reservoir in less than a mile. After this, continue on the track as it begins to bear to the left, following an arm of the reservoir. After another gate the track leaves the valley and crosses pastures, passing the junction of the footpath for Nicky Nook at (4). After this, the trail reaches the farm road for Fell End, coming in from the right. Back on tarmac, after another 300yds you will reach a lane junction.

(5) Turn left and keep on the lane for over a mile to reach the junction with Snowhill Lane.

(6) Turn right. The village centre is reached in a little under ¾ mile from here.

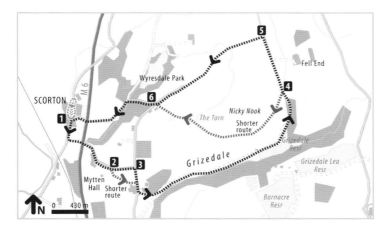

WALKING ROUTE

The tramper trail makes a decent walk but this would miss out on Nicky Nook, one the great viewpoints of Lancashire. Follow the Tramper Trail to:

② Turn right onto a footpath 400yds after the motorway bridge, just past a left bend in the lane. This leads to a stone stile to the left of a cattle grid. This footpath cuts a corner, taking you diagonally left over two large fields (after a small paddock) to reach Higher Lane. When you reach it, turn right. Re-joining the tramper trail, keep on it to:

④ Here, turn left over a stile close to a metal gate. At first, a substantial track leads upwards towards a prominent pillar on the skyline. From the pillar keep ahead to a wall and then follow the path to the trig point. The way down is clear – the path drops to the right on a broad grassy track with a tarn on the right. At a wall corner, turn left and continue the descent to a kissing gate. From here the downward path is particularly steep. Now you will be reunited with the tramper route at ⑥ .

Further information

The Forest of Bowland AONB publishes a leaflet, *Wyresdale Wheels – Access for All*, which gives information about trails around Scorton (see also www.forestofbowland.com).

Thieveley Pike

START Close to The Ram, Cliviger, BB10 4SU, SD875285

DISTANCE 5 miles (8km)

SUMMARY Strenuous to the Pike and then easy

MAP OS Explorer OL21 South Pennines

WHERE TO EAT AND DRINK The Ram, www.theramburnley.co.uk, To1282-459091. Parking is not easy in Holme Chapel so it may be an idea to combine a walk with a visit to the inn (readers should seek permission before the walk)

This thrilling ascent provides everything a walker desires – a sense of challenge, wide spaces and tremendous views.

1 From The Ram continue along the A646 towards Todmorden for almost 500yds. Just past a bus stop, turn right onto a woodland drive leading down to a large house. As the drive swings left, keep ahead on a track leading down to a footbridge. Follow the path along a walled section to a kissing gate leading out on a grassy hillside. Turn right to climb the path steeply. The path is clear and well waymarked. After 300yds it reaches a path junction on a broad shelf below Thieveley Scout.

2 Bear right (ignoring a waymark post pointing left) and follow a low wall gently climbing above Fishpond Plantation to the right, soon with a wall/fence on the right. After 500yds the path meets the Burnley Way on the far side of a deep gully to the left. Turn left through a wooden gate and follow the path steeply up, with a fence to the left. After a track the path becomes less steep and less clear but, maintaining the same direction, keep climbing until the trig point comes into sight.

3 Cross the fence by a ruined wall at a stile to the left of the trig point. Turn right and follow the fence and wall north-westwards along the broad moorland ridge. After 800yds the track crosses a stream at the top of Black Clough and then continues to a gate at a junction of walls. Through this, keep ahead until you arrive at a wooden gate just before the A671 Bacup Rd.

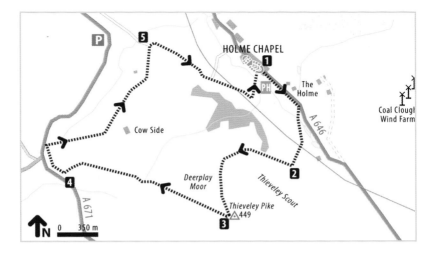

④ Turn right onto the Pennine Bridleway. After passing through a wooden gate, the track heads briefly north before swinging east above Easden Clough on a broad farm road. Before reaching a gate, turn left, following the way below the farm at Cow Side. This puts you on a broad green lane. Keep on this to a point where it turns left in front of a wooden gate. Go through the gate (close to a memorial to Mary Towneley), turn left and on a steeper path head downhill with a fence to the left. As you near a farm, join a farm track to reach a junction with the Burnley Way.

⑤ At a finger post, turn right. Keep on a broad track to reach Scout Farm. After the farm the trail continues parallel to the railway before passing underneath it close to Buckley Wood. Soon after this, turn left on a broad track leading to Holme Chapel.

Points of interest

Opposite The Ram, the churchyard of St John the Divine is the last resting place of General Scarlett, who led the less celebrated, though successful, Charge of the Heavy Brigade at the Battle of Balaclava.

Warton Crag

START Nature Reserve car park, LA5 9SB (nearby), SD492723

DISTANCE 5 miles (8km)

SUMMARY Apart from the obvious ascent of 500ft, the rest of the walk is relatively easy

MAP OS Explorer OL7 The English Lakes: South-eastern area

WHERE TO EAT AND DRINK Two pubs in Warton are The George Washington, www.georgewashingtonwarton.co.uk, T01524-732865; and The Malt Shovel, T01524-874149

Warton Crag is the Lake District's introduction card. On the southern edge of the Arnside & Silverdale Area of Outstanding Natural Beauty, its rocky prominence attracts the eye as you drive north of Lancaster on the M6.

1 Take the footpath to the right of the car park entrance. From a large limestone bench on the right, the path follows a wall parallel to the lane to reach a second entrance close to an information board. From here, bear left up through trees to a kissing gate. Go through this and turn left, climbing steadily up along the edge of the crag. Ten minutes of steady climbing will bring you to a fence above the car park. To reach the summit, cross the fence and look for a narrow path on your right. Follow this to a stile below a rocky shelf. Beyond this, a short scramble will keep you on a path bringing you to a beacon and trig point.

2 With the beacon and trig point on your right, follow the path to a signpost in the woods. Take the direction for Crag Foot. On reaching a wooden gate, turn left. This track will bring you to Crag Rd. Turn right.

3 At the next junction, follow a footpath sign for Coach Road. In 150yds turn right along a track, and past a field turn left into woodland. The way now is up. Pass through a metal gate into pasture. Follow the path until you reach a forbidding 'Private No Footpath' sign. Here, bear left through a gate and follow a faint path. When you reach a metal gate, cross a stile and bear right. After crossing pasture,

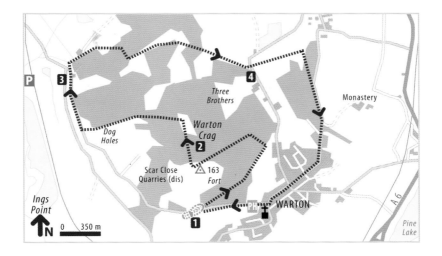

following intermittent waymarked posts to a stone stile, bear left along an improving track.

④ At Peter Lane cross to a squeeze stile and walk up to a metal gate. Keep on the path as it passes a lime kiln and drops into woodland. With a wall on your right, look for a wooden gate marking an entrance into Hyning Scout Wood. Almost immediately inside the wood the path forks. Keep left, descending gently through the trees. When you reach a broader track, bear right. Following the base of a rocky shelf, you will arrive at a track with Warton in view across a field. Here, turn left to reach Hyning Rd. Turn right and walk into the village. After the post office turn right into Crag Rd by The George Washington pub. After 50yds turn right into a small car park and exit rear. Ascend, with an impressive limestone cliff on the right, through a wall to a path junction. Here, bear left to return to the car park using the outward route.

Points of interest

Warton claims links with the family of George Washington, the first US president, hence the name of the pub and the fact that every 4 July the Stars and Stripes is flown from the top of St Oswald's Church.

START Letcliff Hill Country
Park, BB18 5HE, SD879457

DISTANCE 5 miles (8km)

SUMMARY Mainly farm tracks with
some moorland footpaths. The ascent
is gradual and not too strenuous

MAP OS Explorer OL21
South Pennines

Weets Hill, near Barnoldswick (or 'Barlick' to locals), is about as far east as you
can go in Lancashire without straying across the border. It is sometimes referred
to as 'The Third Peak of Pendle' and, although not as high as Pendle Hill or
Boulsworth, it is a superb viewpoint, rewarding all the effort taken to reach it.

1 For the first part of the walk you will be on the Pendle Way, with
its distinctive waymark sign of a witch on a broomstick. Return to
Manchester Rd and turn right, and then after 200yds turn left down
Gillian's Lane. This leads past Bancroft Mill, which is now a museum.
Keep ahead, turning left into Moorgate Rd which leads on to Folly
Lane, a farm track.

2 The ascent now begins. After 500yds look for a gate on the right.
Cross this into pasture and continue the ascent, at first through fields,
but as you gain height across moorland. A stone wall on your left
will now provide a good guide nearly all the way to the top. After
1 mile from the lane the path bears right to reach a trig point at 397m
(or 1,250ft in old money). On a clear day the views are outstanding.

3 Begin a gentle descent, bearing left so you regain the wall, and
follow this down to where it meets a lane end (Gisburn Old Rd). Still
on the Pendle Way, turn left and walk past Weets House. Keep on the
lane for the next mile. Just beyond Star Hall you will part company
with the Pendle Way, which bears off to the right.

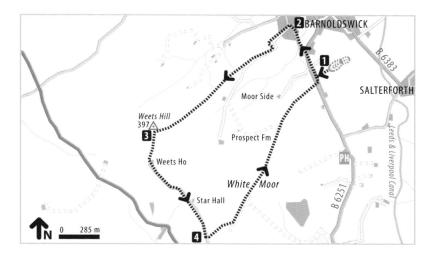

(4) After Star Hall take the first footpath on the left. This crosses three fields to reach Lister Well Rd, which is not a road at all but a rough track. On reaching it, turn left to commence a long straight descent back to the B625 on a gradually improving surface. At the road, turn left for the car park, which on a clear day you would have spotted from some considerable distance away.

Points of interest

Bancroft Mill (www.bancroftmill.org.uk) opened in 1920 and produced high quality cotton cloths. At peak production it manufactured 200,000yds of cloth a week. When it closed in 1978, plans were made for its demolition until a group of enthusiasts came forward with a proposal to preserve part of the site – in particular the engine, engine house, boiler rooms and chimney – as a museum dedicated to the cotton industry. The Bancroft Mill Engine Trust was set up in 1980 and continues to thrive, opening up for steam days on Saturdays throughout the spring and summer.

The Brock Valley & Beacon Fell

START Brock Valley picnic site
car park, PR3 0PF, SD549431

DISTANCE 5½ miles (9km)

SUMMARY Mainly easy,
with one steep climb

MAP OS Explorer OL41
Forest of Bowland

A lovely and varied walk that crosses one of Lancashire's most popular country parks.

[1]   Turn right along White Lee Lane. Keep on it for 15mins to reach Bleasdale Lane. Here, turn right then left onto a footpath that leads up through fields to reach Beacon Fell Country Park. When you reach the fell road, keep ahead on a broad track leading to the Visitors' Centre. Continue, with the car park on your right, along a well laid trail. At the next junction of paths turn left in a northerly direction and soon you will reach the open moorland and the trig point.

[2]   Keep ahead on a good path that drops towards woodland. When it joins a wide track, turn left. On reaching a wooden sculpture, turn right. The track leads down through densely planted conifers to reach the fell road. Cross and take the footpath diagonally opposite. After a stile go straight to a junction of paths. Turn right then walk along a grassy track to a stile next to a wooden gate before a farm. After crossing it, turn left and walk down to the tarmac lane.

[3]   At the lane turn right and follow it to Wickens Barn. Just beyond it, turn left onto a footpath that skirts its grounds. With the fence on your left, keep ahead to reach a stile by a metal gate on the left. Cross into the adjoining field and continue in the same direction, now with the fence on your right. Enter a patch of woodland, cross a stile and drop down to a lane. Turn left. This scattered community is Bleasdale. Close to houses on the left, turn right onto the estate road and bear

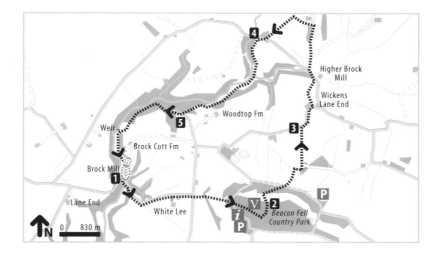

left at a Y junction. In 600yds, just before the primary school, turn left onto another well maintained road. After 200yds reach a footpath on the left. Take this in a diagonal direction to cross pastureland to Weavers Farm. When you reach the lane, turn right but look for a footpath on the opposite side of the lane leading up the embankment.

④ Follow this to edge alongside woodland above the River Brock, with a fence on your left. At the first stile in the fence cross it and continue with the fence on your right. The path takes you to the bottom of the valley and then keep ahead until you reach Waddecar Scout Activity Centre. Keep on the main track as it leads past an Archery Range, then toilets on the left. Where the main track swings left up a deep gully, the footpath continues ahead, past a barrier gate and through a small field. Beyond the field the path re-enters the woods and crosses a footbridge. Soon after, it joins a bridleway on a bend. This takes you up to Snape Rake Lane, a narrow tarmac lane.

⑤ Turn right. The tarmac soon peters out as the track descends back to the river. Before reaching a footbridge, turn left. After 200yds the path comes to open ground with a white building ahead. The track passes this on its left to reach a more substantial lane. Bear left slightly uphill. After the track levels out, take a path on the back towards the river. With the river on the right, follow the footpath back to Brock Mill.

START Burscough Bridge
Interchange, L40 0SA, SD444124

DISTANCE 5½ miles (9km)

SUMMARY Very easy

MAP OS Explorer 285
Southport & Chorley

WHERE TO EAT AND DRINK
The Martin Inn, T01704-892095,
and The Farmers Arms,
T01704-896021, are both en route

USEFUL WEBSITE
www.wwt.org.uk
for the Wildfowl and Wetlands Trust

This walk out on the flatlands of west Lancashire visits the internationally
important Martin Mere Wetland Centre.

1   From the station walk back to the A59 and turn left and then,
once across the bridge, left again into Red Cat Lane. A short distance
from Liverpool Rd follow a footpath sign on the left. This leads you
to a narrow path alongside the railway and a dedicated trail to Martin
Mere. For 600yds follow the railway until you come to Crabtree Lane
close to a level crossing. Turn right. Stay on Crabtree Lane for 500yds
and then, when the lane turns sharply left, follow it to the next corner.
Here, following the signpost, turn left onto a farm track. Bear right in
front of a cottage and then turn right on a path leading across open
arable fields to Marsh Moss Lane. Opposite as you reach the lane is
a concessionary path leading to the chain link fence that marks the
perimeter of Martin Mere Wildfowl and Wetlands Trust reserve.

2   To enter the reserve, turn right (admission fees apply). To
continue the walk, keep ahead with the perimeter fence on your right.
The footpath crosses a track connecting the Harrier Hide on the left
and the reserve. It continues beyond the reserve onto the vast prairie
of west Lancashire. After 200yds the track bends to the left alongside
a large pool. After a wooden gate keep ahead on a less defined path
following a sluice. This leads to a footpath sign indicating right. Turn
right, aiming for a rather worn farm building 200yds away. When
you reach it, turn left onto a track that leads across the railway and

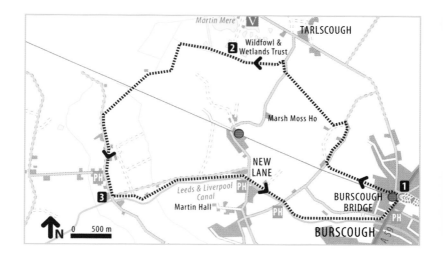

continues towards Derby Farm. When you reach the lane, turn left. Continue to the junction of Merscar Lane and keep ahead past the Martin Inn.

③ Now on Martin Lane, walk down to its junction with Gorst Lane and then turn left to join the towpath of the Leeds–Liverpool Canal. Keep on it until you reach Burscough. Exit at the A59 and turn left for the station.

Points of interest

The Wildfowl and Wetlands Trust is the creation of Sir Peter Scott (1909–89). Naturalist, wildlife artist, war hero, broadcaster, author, sailor and glider pilot, he developed the notion of 'bringing wildlife and people together for the benefit of both' and in 1946 set up a wildfowl reserve at Slimbridge, Gloucestershire. From here, the WWT expanded to manage nine centres in total, including Martin Mere. Little wonder that Sir Peter has been called the most influential conservationist of the twentieth century. He opened Martin Mere in 1975.

START Clough Head car park,
Haslingden Grane, BB4 4AT, SD751231

DISTANCE 5½ miles (9km)

SUMMARY Moderate
verging on strenuous

MAP OS Explorer 287
West Pennine Moors

WHERE TO EAT AND DRINK
The Visitors' Centre and café at
Clough Head, T07973-878821

This route takes you up to the moors above Calf Hey Reservoir to the distinctive
summit of Hog Lowe Pike.

[1] Taking the footpath to the left of the entrance drive, walk back
to the Grane Rd and cross it. This happens to be the most dangerous
part of the walk. Although designated a B road, most drivers seem
to be under the impression they are on the M6. Once safely across,
turn left and in a short distance pass through a kissing gate leading
into woodland. Follow the path as it leads downhill to reach Calf Hey
Reservoir car park. (An alternative start, but this car park has no toilet
facilities.)

Turn right and continue on the service road through the car park
and keep ahead to the next junction (a footpath close to the pay and
display machine arrives at this same point). Turn right. The road
leads round past ruined farms to gently descend to a bridge at the top
end of Calf Hey Reservoir. Cross the bridge and turn left, following a
shoreline track which crosses one feeder stream and then turns right
onto a narrow path just before a second stream. After 150yds cross
the stream at a footbridge and start to climb steeply through a conifer
plantation. After reaching a shelf, the path bears right and continues
through the steep-sided woods to arrive at the edge of moorland.
From this point the first objective, Hog Lowe Pike, will be visible
across to the right. The path follows a fence and then dips to cross a
gully before crossing moorland to reach the trig point just after a stile.

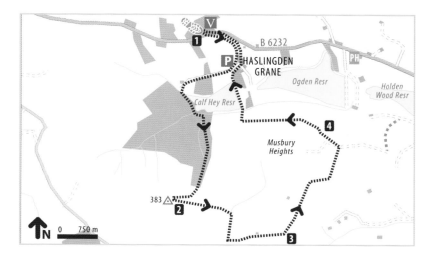

(2) The next section of the walk is a moorland yomp over Causeway Height. From the trig point follow the fence you have just crossed towards a corner east of the trig point. After negotiating three stiles in quick succession (one on the left and then two ahead), maintain the easterly direction with a fence on the right. After 300yds turn right at a corner and keep ahead to reach another corner. Turn left and take a path that crosses diagonally to a wall, passing through a gap when you reach it. The path drops off the heights into Musbury Valley and intercepts the Rossendale Way at a wall corner.

(3) Turn left, aiming towards an isolated tree close to ruins. Keep on the broad peaty track as it contours in a northerly direction. After crossing a stream, the Way passes through an area of disused workings, the most obvious feature of which is a tall stand-alone chimney.

(4) When you reach the chimney, follow the path right through ruins to the edge of a steep escarpment overlooking Ogden Reservoir. Bear left on a steep rocky path leading below Musbury Heights. After the path levels out, turn right onto a path that takes you down to the dam end of Calf Hey Reservoir. Cross the broad end of the dam and follow the road opposite to reach the junction on your outward route.

Start Marles Wood car
park and picnic area, PR3
3XR (nearby), SD676356

Distance 5½ miles (9km)

Summary Easy walking
over farmland

Map OS Explorer 287
West Pennine Moors

A gentle stroll in the Ribble Valley with fine views of Pendle.

① Return to the lane and turn right, walking downhill to the first
bend. Cross a stile on the left and follow a footpath leading uphill,
at first alongside trees but after a stile diagonally right across fields.
As the path levels out, turn right at a wire fence and continue to a
junction of footpaths at a corner close to a large ash tree. Here, turn
left over a wooden stile and continue along a track to reach a large
farm. Keep ahead through the yard and continue along its drive to
arrive at Copster Green.

② The Green is bisected by the busy A59. When you reach the
road, turn left and then after 200yds left again onto the drive leading
towards Copster Hall. Continue on the drive as it crosses a cattle
grid and passes a barn to reach a sprawling small holding. Here, bear
right to cross a stile next to a metal gate. In the field beyond bear left,
crossing a large field and then dropping to a wooden footbridge over
Park Brook. Across this, climb up to an isolated stone stile and then
keep ahead, at first following the remains of an old dry stone wall, to a
wooden stile in the left field corner. In the next field, which is marshy,
aim for the gable end of a property at Dinckley Grange to the right.
As you come near to it, cross a stile onto the lawn and then join the
drive leading past the grand house. As the drive bears left and before it

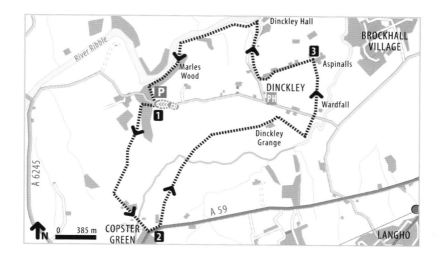

reaches the lane, turn right onto a path leading into a large field. Keep ahead for 400yds, then as the way begins to drop towards Park Brook turn left, crossing a stile next to the brook in the left-hand field corner. Cross the field and a stile into the lane, turn right and immediately left onto the drive of another imposing property. After passing the barn on the right, go through a wooden gate and continue over the next field, aiming towards the left of Aspinall's Farm ahead. The path dips to a plank bridge and then traverses three fields to bring you alongside the main house.

③   Follow the path to the left of the farm to cross a new stile into a lane. Turn left and keep on this for 500yds to reach a junction. Here, turn right onto a private road leading down to Dinckley Hall. Pass the main entrance to the hall itself and, when you can proceed no further, turn left onto a path that drops down to the river close by the impressive suspension bridge. The way continues past the bridge (not across it), with the river on your right. After crossing waterside pastures, the path enters Marles Wood; after 500yds turns upwards for the car park.

62

63

Rivington & Winter Hill

START/FINISH Rivington Hall Barn, Rivington, BL6 7SB, SD633144

DISTANCE Short route 2 miles (3.2km); long route 5½ miles (9km)

SUMMARY The short route is an ideal family outing, taking you to a fine viewpoint and back through the Terraced Gardens; the long route is a more serious and demanding expedition

MAP OS Explorer 287 West Pennine Moors

WHERE TO EAT AND DRINK The Great House Barn Tea room, www.rivingtonhallbarn.co.uk, T01204-697738

The main transmitter mast on Winter Hill, at 1,013ft (309m), is Lancashire's most prominent landmark. This walk takes you right up close and personal to the tower on a route with several other points of interest.

1 From the car park follow the lane to the left of the main entrance, which quickly leads into woodland. Keep on the main track as it leads up to a gate and crosses pastureland to enter the wooded slopes of the Terraced Gardens. Thread your way through the gardens until you reach the upper track (known as the Belmont Rd). From here the way to Rivington Pike will become obvious – it is adorned with a tower. If this is all you want to do, then you have achieved the main objective of the short route. From here, in returning to the car park enjoy a more leisurely exploration of the Terraced Gardens.

2 For those determined to complete the long route, the way to Winter Hill is clear – well over a mile of moorland walking heading north-west, following at times a boggy track but with some stone slabbing to reach the impressive main mast. When you reach the service road beyond the mast, turn left.

3 Continue on the service road as it turns to the left, passing several other masts and service buildings to reach the trig point. This height is one of the most well-known in the north-west of England, but few people have ever walked up to it. From the trig point continue on the

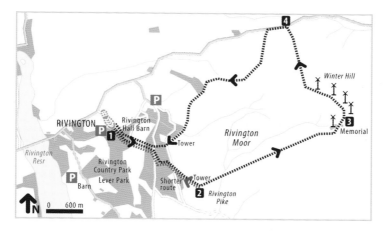

service road and then, as it ends, bear right onto a footpath that drops steeply alongside a fence to the Belmont Rd, reaching the top of the pass known as Hordern Stoops.

4 When you reach the road, turn left and keep on it for 300yds before turning left onto a broad stoned track (the Belmont Rd). Walking briskly for 30mins will bring you to the base of the Pigeon Tower, Lady Leverhulme's place of quiet retreat.

From here, thread your way down through the Terraced Gardens and back to the car.

The traverse across Rivington Moor can be excessively boggy after wet weather. If you don't fancy it, drop to the south, picking up a track leading back to the Belmont Rd. Turn left. Keep ahead to Pike Cottage (first building on the left). Here, turn left onto a footpath leading uphill. Where it divides, bear right to visit the three cairns on the hill marked cryptically as 'Two Lads'. Continue on the path to intercept the service road. Turn left for the summit.

Points of interest

The Terraced Gardens was once the home of William Leverhulme, creator of the multinational giant, Lever Brothers, and at the start of the twentieth century one of the wealthiest men in the world.

START Witton Country Park, main entrance car park, BB2 2TP, SD662271

DISTANCE 5½ miles (9km)

SUMMARY Mainly gentle field and woodland walking

MAP OS Explorer 287 West Pennine Moors

This walk follows a section of the Witton Weavers Way – Beamers Trail – which starts at Witton Park.

1 From the car park walk towards the running track and sports pavilion. Just beyond these amenities the path enters a wooded area. Before the visitors' centre turn right on a path that takes you past a lily pond. At Big Carr Wood turn left. As the path leads upwards it forks in a little less than 200yds. Take the left fork across a brook and follow with the edge of the wood on your left. Leave the wood by a kissing gate and cross two fields to enter a lane.

2 Turn left and take a bridleway on the right into the woods of Billinge Hill. Keep on the track to reach a small car park. Cross the car park to follow a footpath that crosses pastureland to put you above a disused quarry. The path descends to a corner to the left of a property; on reaching the lane turn left. Almost immediately enter woodland, turning onto a public footpath on the right. This drops down gently to reach a junction of paths. Here, turn right and quickly arrive at a low stile leading to a field. Keep ahead on the path with field boundaries where they exist on the right. After 700yds you come to a lane (Pleasington Rd). Cross the road onto a footpath that crosses two fields to bring you to Close Farm. Turn left.

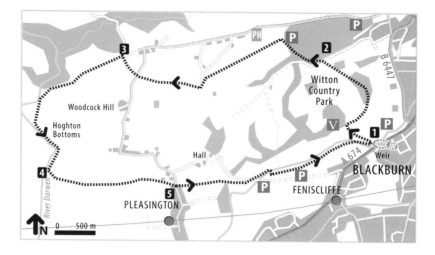

(3) Keep to the right of the house and, on entering the field beyond, bear left at the end of a wall to pass through a gap. Keep ahead with a hedge on your right. The path descends across a depression to a stile in a wall. After crossing a gully, the path follows a wire fence on the right for 700yds. The path drops down, past a scout hut, to river level, passing through the garden of a farmhouse. Just before a footbridge crossing to Hoghton Bottoms, turn left along a broad track. With the river on your right, follow it to a stone bridge.

(4) At the bridge turn left onto a track leading gently upwards. When the trail meets a wall, turn left and then cross a stile to enter broken woodland on the edge of Pleasington golf course. On leaving the course, keep ahead to the left of a fence leading uphill. As the path levels out, keep ahead until a stile is reached that gives out onto a track in front of an imposing thatched house. You now enter a modern development and soon after reach Pleasington.

(5) Cross the lane and continue forward on a path that is fenced on both sides. After crossing a sandy area the path descends to a lane, bringing you to the edge of the extensive playing fields that lead down to Witton Park. Head for the bridge, cross it and continue with the river on your left. The way back to the car park will be obvious from this point.

WALK

65 Chipping

START Chipping village car
park, PR3 2QH, SD621432

DISTANCE 6 miles (9.7km)

SUMMARY Moderate

MAP OS Explorer OL41
Forest of Bowland

WHERE TO EAT AND DRINK
The Cobble Corner Café,
www.thecobblecorner.co.uk,
T01995-61551;
The Sun Inn,
www.thesuninnchipping.co.uk,
T01995-61206;
The Tillotsons Arms,
www.thetillotsonsarms.co.uk,
T01995-61568

A walk from one of Lancashire's loveliest villages, which is located on the edge of the Forest of Bowland AONB.

① From the car park turn left onto Church Raike. When the lane forks, bear right to dip down to a new housing estate (built on the site of an old mill). Keep ahead to reach a mill pond on the left. Part way along, turn right onto a footpath that leads steeply uphill. At first, keep the field boundary on your right but after a stile bear left, passing beneath telephone wires to follow a path that begins to drop down to a brook. After a stile the path reaches a footbridge and then commences a climb, first to a farmyard at Windy Hill where it turns right and then immediately left, then continues for a further 600yds with the field boundary on the right. As the way levels and before reaching a low hill, turn left and cross to a stile, aiming towards the rounded form of Burnslack Fell. Across the stile, bear right towards pine trees.

② Cross a stile onto a farm road and turn immediately right onto a broad track. Go through a gate. Keep on the track for almost a mile as it crosses a stretch of moorland to arrive at Lickhurst Farm. At the farm bear left onto the farm road and follow it downhill and then to the right. In 500yds it arrives at a junction with a lane, passing an isolated telephone box.

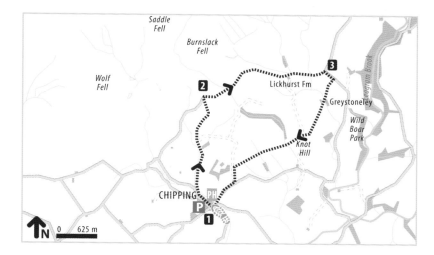

③   Turn right at the junction and then right onto the drive of Higher Greystoneley. Follow the track as it passes through the complex and then descends to a wooded clough. After a footbridge climb up to reach Lower Greystoneley. On an improving track, keep ahead for almost 500yds past Knot Barn to arrive at Knot Hill. Turn right and then follow the base of the hill on your left. As you reach its far side keep ahead across a field to reach a double stile in the hedgerow. Beyond this, the path dips down to a footbridge and climbs the steep-sided valley with the fence line to the right. In 500yds the path crosses a stream and then soon after enters the wide open space of parkland near Leagram Hall. Keep ahead until you reach a drive. Turn left and follow the drive to the lane. Turn right for Chipping. When you reach the village, turn right into the main street.

START Churchtown village centre, PR3 0HT, SD482429

DISTANCE 6 miles (9.7km)

SUMMARY Easy – almost entirely on the flat

MAP OS Explorer OL41 Forest of Bowland

WHERE TO EAT AND DRINK There are several excellent restaurants and pubs in Garstang – just beyond the Wyre Aqueduct. At the end (or beginning) of the walk is the Punchbowl Inn (T01995-603360) and Horns Inn (T01995-601351). Sample local cheeses at Dewlay Farm Shop, www.dewlay.com, T01995-602335

This route is promoted as the Crumbly Lancashire Cheese Trail, as it passes close to the largest cheese producer in Lancashire – Dewlay, on the edge of Garstang. It is a delightful walk full of interest.

1️⃣ From Church St follow the lane pass the market pillar to St Helen's Church. In the far corner of the car park take a path that leads to a suspension footbridge across the River Wyre. After crossing the river, turn left onto a path to Catterall.

2️⃣ Turn right onto Old Lancaster Rd and then after 100yds left, passing between buildings to arrive on the A6. Cross to Tan Yard Rd and, after passing the large works site, turn left onto a riverside footpath that edges along railings before continuing to the left of a housing estate to reach playing fields. Keep ahead to Garstang Rd (B6430). Turn left to cross Calder Bridge and then turn right over a stile. Keep to the hedgerow on the left for 500yds to reach a farm lane. Turn right to follow it to Sturzaker House. As you reach the complex, turn left on a private road. When you reach the canal (accessed by a gate on the right), turn left on its towpath.

3️⃣ For the next 45mins put away these directions and relax to enjoy this delightful reach of the Lancaster Canal as it contours through the pleasant countryside close to Garstang. Turn left 50yds after the Wyre Aqueduct onto a footpath through a wooden gate.

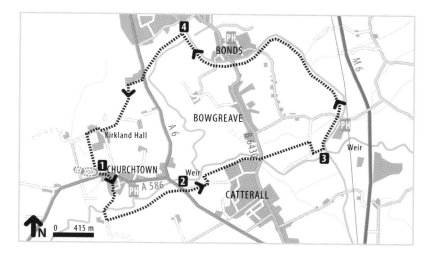

4 Once more on the Wyre Way, follow the well waymarked path as it takes you across fields to the A6. As you near the A6 the path swings away from the riverside to climb an embankment to reach the road. Turn left and then, at a footpath sign, turn right to the drive of Cross House Farm. Keep ahead through the yard and continue with woodland on the right. When you reach a junction at a metal gate, bear left onto a gravelly track. Ahead, the huge wind turbine of Dewlay provides feature on the flat landscape. In 400yds, where the track turns left, keep ahead through a metal gate and then cross the field to its far right corner. After a stile bear right on a track leading round Kirkland Hall. After passing through the yard of Kirkland Hall Farm, turn left onto a farm track leading to the A586 Fleetwood Rd. When you reach it, turn left for Churchtown.

Darwen Tower

START Lychgate car park,
Darwen, BB3 1JX, SD679224

DISTANCE 6 miles (9.7km)

SUMMARY Moderate

MAP OS Explorer 287
West Pennine Moors

WHERE TO EAT AND DRINK
The Sunnyhurst, To1254-873035;
The Royal Arms,
http://theroyalarms-tockholes.co.uk,
To1254-705373;
Vaughn's Country Café,
www.vaughnscountrycafe.co.uk ,
To1254-705373

USEFUL WEBSITE
www.blackburn.gov.uk for details
about Sunnyhurst Woods, well
worth exploring in their own right

Darwen Tower is a well recognized landmark for travellers on the M65. This walk
takes you up to this superb viewpoint and explores the moors and woodlands
nearby.

1 From the car park pass the Sunnyhurst pub and then turn right
onto a bridleway leading past houses onto Darwen Moor. Soon the
scale of the climb becomes obvious, with the Tower prominent on the
skyline. Keep on the main track until you reach it.

2 To continue the walk, take the broad path from the trig point
leading southwards along the edge of Darwen Moor, with the steep
escarpment on your right. After 750yds this reaches a distinctive stone
marker post and the path drops towards a gully. At the next junction,
bear right past the stone marker and bench and continue to a stile.
Cross the stile before descending on a flagged path to reach a broad
track. Turn left and follow it as it loops rightwards through a patch of
woodland.

3 Almost immediately on exiting the trees, turn left over a stile
next to a wooden gate and continue with a wall on the right. The track
leads to the farmstead of New Barn. When you reach the complex,

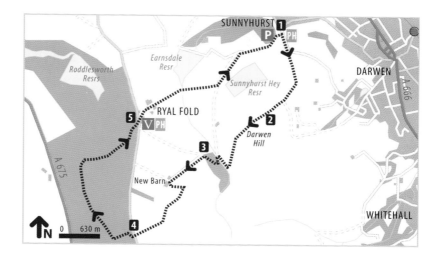

turn left on a track (just before a metal gate) leading up to the moors. This bears left to a gate in the fence, then continues to climb to a broad track. Here, turn right. After passing a second wooden gate, follow this track for almost 400yds to intercept a track coming down from the top of the moor. Turn right and follow it down to Tockholes Rd.

④ Cross a stone stile opposite and turn right. In 200yds turn left in front of Slipper Lowe car park. Go through a gate and follow a broad track to a junction. Turn right. After crossing the brow of Slipper Lowe, the track gently drops on a rough stony track to a wide bridge in a little under 900yds. Do not cross it but take the left of two tracks on the right which climb away from the brook. In another 200yds turn right onto a path which, after crossing a tiny stream, climbs back to Tockholes Rd opposite a car park, information centre and Vaughn's Country Café.

⑤ Turn left. Immediately after the Royal Arms follow a footpath on the right that comes out at Ryal Fold. After passing a farmhouse take the waymarked gate on the right and cross the paddock to the field beyond. The path is not distinct so bear right as you drop to cross Stepback Brook, close to the tip of Earnsdale Reservoir. The way rises to cross two fields to bring you on a track below Sunnyhurst Hey Reservoir. Turn left. This track leads down to the upper car park of Sunnyhurst Park.

Gressingham

START Gressingham, close to the church of St John the Evangelist, LA2 8LP, SD572699

DISTANCE 6 miles (9.7km)

SUMMARY Easy

MAPS OS Explorer OL7 The English Lakes: South-eastern area, and OS Explorer OL41 Forest of Bowland

A mainly riverside walk in the mid Lune Valley.

① From the church of St John the Evangelist walk down to cross a stone bridge and turn right. Within 100m turn left onto a footpath, taking you through the garden of Crowtrees. Cross to a stone stile over a wall and then follow the path, at first slightly right, up to an awkward stile by a tree in the corner and then up to a double stile. After you cross the brow of the hill, bear right to skirt through the yard of Eskrigge Farm and then follow its drive to the lane.

② Turn left. Now on Eskrigge Lane, walk along it for 100yds and then turn right onto a short lane, soon leading to an overgrown green lane. The path eventually leads slightly uphill and then after a stile reaches open fields. Keep ahead on a waymarked path with the hedge on the left. At the next gate cross a stile and, with a fence on the right, head downhill. After two more stiles the path passes to the left of a barn and reaches a wooded lane. Turn left. Within 100yds turn left onto a footpath, which is in fact the Lune Valley Ramble.

③ Taking a course more or less at right angles to the lane you've just left will bring you to a stile in a fence. Cross this and now with the river in sight on your right enjoy a 3-mile easy walk upstream to Arkholme. (Alternatively take a footpath that follows the left-hand edge of the fields on the flood plain until you intercept the riverside path.) After 1½ miles the route crosses the road close by Loyn Bridge.

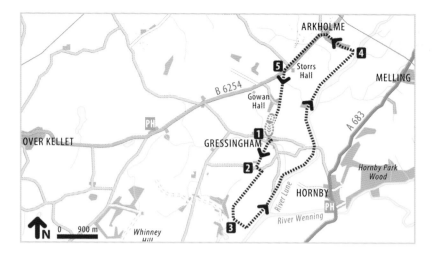

4   As you near Arkholme, pass a white cottage on the left before entering a wooded corner. Here, take the track leading left into the village. The route continues straight up through the village until you reach the crossroads with the B6254   Turn left. It will be best to cross the road and walk on the right as the pavement soon runs out. Keep on the road for a mile, passing Locka Lane on the right and Storrs Hall on the left.

5   Just beyond the Hall entrance, as the road reaches woodland, turn left onto a path accessed by a green door. As the path reaches open fields, bear right and follow the path as it crosses three fields to reach a lane. Here, turn left for Gressingham.

Points of interest

As you reach Arkholme, the chapel is tucked away on the right almost immediately as you leave the river. A notice inside will inform you that Arkholme is in fact 'A Thankful Village', where all its young men serving in the armed forces during the 1914–18 war returned home. Surprisingly, given the carnage of the conflict, there are fifty-two villages in England and Wales identified as such. There are none in Scotland or Northern Ireland.

START Small lay-by car park on the corner of Startifants Lane, 2 miles north of Chipping, PR3 2NP (nearby), SD601442

DISTANCE 6 miles (9.7km)

SUMMARY Strenuous; in mist the route will need good navigational skills

MAP OS Explorer OL41 Forest of Bowland

A classic round in the Forest of Bowland Area of Outstanding Natural Beauty.

① Follow the steep lane towards Parlick. At Fell Foot – the isolated farmhouse – go through a gate onto the fellside. The way is now up to the summit (1,417ft/432m), indicated by a ragged cairn. The way ahead to Fair Snape opens out. Here, a helpful fence will serve as a handrail for the first part of this trek. The way drops gently from Parlick, then, after crossing an awkward nick, begins to rise with a wall on the right. The summit (1,673ft/510m) is adorned by a large cairn that supports a feature called Paddy's Pole, which is in fact … a pole. Nearby there is something of a shelter and a trig point. The views are extensive.

② If the day is clear, it will be possible to pick out a junction of fences at a distance of 700yds on the skyline to the north-east. With Paddy's Pole to your right and the trig point on your left, aim towards this feature. A path of sorts will lead you through peat hags to a fence to the right. The fence will lead you to the junction of fences, with a kissing gate just before the highest part of the fell (1,706ft/520m) marked by an unimpressive cairn. Prior to 2013 you would be faced with a sticky plod over a stile and through soggy peat to the summit. Now, however, a flagged path laid as part of a moorland conservation scheme will lead you dry shod to the summit.

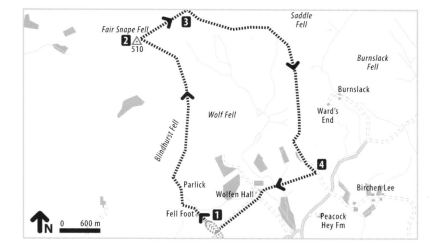

3 Having visited the cairn, return to the kissing gate and follow a path leading slightly downhill. At a distance of 50yds from the kissing gate, the track divides at a small cairn. Here, turn left. Walking becomes progressively easier along the track, which leads to another kissing gate and Saddle Fell. Once on Saddle Fell, follow the downward track heading south. After a stile next to a gate, a more pastoral landscape opens up. Follow the track down to Saddle End Farm.

4 Through the farmyard, turn sharp right, cross a stile and follow the path between two fences within a stand of trees. The next stile gives out onto open pasture. Using waymark posts, keep ahead, crossing into another field and then dropping into a deep valley. Cross Chipping Brook by way of a footbridge, and follow the path to emerge from the valley on a field corner near Wolfen Hall. The right of way passes around this farm/holiday accommodation complex to the left. Waymark signs will keep you on the route. Once on the farm road, you'll quickly arrive at the lane end.

Sawley ▶

START Sawley, close to the Spread
Eagle Hotel, BB7 4NH, SD776465

DISTANCE 6 miles (9.7km)

SUMMARY Moderate; from Grindleton
there is a steady ascent to Beacon Hill

MAP OS Explorer OL41
Forest of Bowland

WHERE TO EAT AND DRINK
The Spread Eagle, Sawley,
www.spreadeaglesawley.co.uk,
T01200-441202

This route has it all – a pleasant riverside amble, gentle pastureland, conifer
woodland and one of the finest viewpoints in the north of England.

(1)   From the hotel walk along the road to Sawley Bridge and cross
the River Ribble. On the far side turn left onto a footpath that crosses
to Sawley Rd. When you reach it, turn left and continue along the
lane, passing Bowland High School on the right. Where the road
bends sharply to the right, take a farm track on the right towards Hey.
Before you reach the farm, take a footpath on the left. Keeping to the
hedgerow on the left, this crosses several fields to reach a farm track.
Turn left. This leads to Grindleton. After passing a chapel, turn right
on Main St.

(2)   Walk up through the village, reaching Top of Town. Here, on the
edge of Grindleton, turn left into White Hall Lane onto a bridleway.
This leads round to the farm complex of White Hall. As you reach it,
turn right onto a farm track and continue for another 500yds until you
reach Cob House.

(3)   Still on the bridleway, keep ahead and after 200yds bear right
following the track with a wall on the left. This leads onto open
moorland. Keep on the track until you reach a metalled lane. Turn left.

(4)   Five mins' walk (400yds) will bring you past two houses.
Immediately after the second drive, turn right onto a forest track.
After curving left, turn right onto a footpath close to an isolated oak

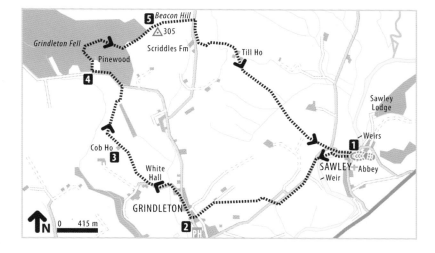

tree on the right of the track. Follow this up the hillside beside a wall.
Cross a former forestry track – ignoring the waymark sign indicating
a right turn – continuing up alongside the wall. At a 'Y' path junction,
take the right-hand path that passes between stone walls to reach a
wooden stile. Continue rising between a walled area to a top corner.
Keep ahead across a stile and a metal gate to reach the trig point. The
views are extensive.

⑤ The route continues to the north of the trig point, dropping
to a metal gate. Turn right to follow a gully/ditch across two fields
down to a lane. Turn right. After 200yds turn left onto a footpath that
follows the hedge to the far left corner. Cross a stile, dropping to a
farm lane. Turn left. Follow the lane as it leads round to Till House
and then continues to a large house. Here, the public footpath crosses
the garden on a waymarked trail to reach a stile on its far side. After
this, continue downhill with a fence on the right. On reaching open
pasture, keep ahead to a footbridge. A short way beyond this turn
left through a thick hedge and walk up a rise, aiming for a pair of
stand-alone trees. After crossing the rise, continue to a field corner
and then with a hedgerow on your right. This leads to another patch
of woodland, leading down to the rear of a property close to a lane on
the left. This leads down to Sawley Rd. Turn left for the village.

Whalley

START Spring Wood picnic site near
Whalley, BB7 9DR (nearby), SD740361

DISTANCE 6 miles (9.7km)

SUMMARY Moderate

MAP OS Explorer 287
West Pennine Moors

This walk starts near Whalley and visits Sabden, another of those villages with close associations with the Pendle Witches.

1 From the car park turn left onto Accrington Rd. Walk alongside the golf course to Portfield Rd. Turn left. Walk uphill to the junction with Portfield Lane. Cross to a footpath. Follow this across fields to reach the lane of Easterley Farm. Turn left and then right onto Old Roman Rd. After 350yds turn left onto a farm drive. As you approach the farm keep right onto a footpath that leads into pastureland. Keep ahead through a kissing gate and, after crossing a field, cross a stile to the right of a hedge and then turn left to a metal gate. Through this, turn right to walk up to a riding centre. As the track reaches buildings, follow it right and then U turn left around tall conifers onto a narrow path. As the path opens out on the right, bear right across a paddock, aiming towards a stile. Follow waymark signs taking you past a wind turbine and then close to a wall on your right. Follow the wall to its far corner and turn right, cross the wall and keep ahead to reach Back Lane. Turn left.

2 After 200m turn left onto the farm drive of Whittaker's Farm. Follow the drive as it swings to the right and then continue along a grassy track to cross a stile. This footpath takes you down to Sabden. As it nears the village it joins a bridleway. Close to a playing field, turn left to enter the village. Turn right into Pendleside Close on a bridleway leading to Padiham Rd. Turn left.

3 Walk along the road, heading uphill. After passing Crowtrees

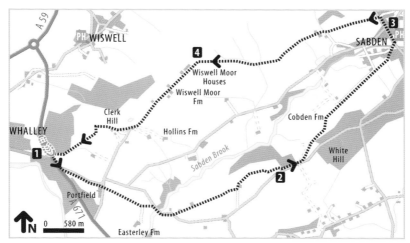

Rd on the right, cross to a footpath on the left. Cross two fields to reach a stone stile. Cross this, turn right and then swing left onto a path leading between buildings. After a pair of metal gates continue on a path that edges along a plantation. Keep ahead after a kissing gate – now in the open with a fence on the right. After the next kissing gate enter a large pasture, bearing right, to begin the climb towards Wiswell Moor. After crossing a gully aim for the fence just below woodland. Here, cross a stile and continue the ascent to another stile. Cross the next pasture to its far left corner. When you reach the track, turn left.

4 Pass Wiswell Moor Farm and continue along a lane for ¾ mile. After passing the drive of Lower Clerk Hill on the left, turn right on a track to Clerk Hill. As you reach the property, turn right by a gate post. Follow the path as it edges around the house. After three stiles turn left – cross another and head downhill with a fence on your left. After 250yds cross a stile and then a footbridge to reach the golf course. Keep ahead with Spring Wood on your right. A stile in the corner will put you in the car park.

START Accrington railway
station, BB5 1LN, SD757285

DISTANCE 6½ miles (10.5km)

SUMMARY Easy

MAP OS Explorer 287
West Pennine Moors

An easy walk from the town centre, leading to a surprising elevation with
outstanding views.

[1]   From the station turn right and then at a roundabout turn left
into Eagle St. Arriving at a development called Waterside, follow the
walkway/cycleway to the left of an artificial lake. This will bring you
onto Mount St. Cross to continue along the Hyndburn Greenway.
After 30mins of walking, Higher Baxenden is reached. Keep on the
cycleway and pass under a bridge to reach a sign indicating the cycle
route (No. 6) turns left towards Lower Baxenden.

[2]   Keep left and take the track left back to the bridge and cross
over the cycleway towards a large house (Alma Place). Pass the
house and bear left onto a farm track. Pass a cottage to the left and
keep ahead through a metal gate into a field. Where the grassy track
divides bear right, climbing the steep hillside alongside a wooded
valley. As the way levels out, keep left to reach a stile at the end of a
wall. With the valley to the left, keep ahead to a stile and then follow
a broad grassy track as it drops to a stream. Cross the slab bridge and
follow the wall opposite to Lark Hill Farm. As you come alongside
the main buildings, turn right on a footpath across a field to reach
Haslingden Rd (B6236).

[3]   Turn right. Keep on the road for half a mile. After passing a
garden centre, turn right at a farm track opposite Tollbar Cottage.
Keep on a broad track as it swings left, passes by tall metal gates and
drops across Accrington Moor. With Green Haworth Golf Course to
the left, keep ahead to a junction of tracks. Turn left.

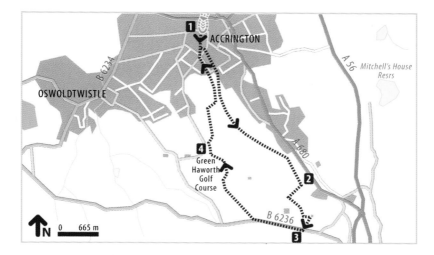

④ After the clubhouse turn right into a farmyard. Bear left between house and barn and then turn right through a metal gate. After two ladder stiles, descend bearing slightly left to a corner in front of a farmhouse. Pass the house on a broad track, which leads towards a terrace of cottages. Just before reaching them, turn right onto a broad track and then immediately left through a yard, keeping to the right of a garden shed. The narrow path leads out to pastures. Keep ahead with a wall on your right. In less than 100yds the path meets another coming in from the right, close to a ruined barn. Here, turn left onto a grassy track. After 350yds of gentle descent turn right on a farm track leading to a stables complex. At the next junction turn left, looking for a footpath sign on the right. The path leads down towards a footbridge across a stream. Do not cross but turn left, and with the stream on your right walk along a wooded path into Accrington. As you emerge from the woods, keep ahead until you reach Mount St. Turn right for the cycleway at the start of the walk.

START Delph Lane, Quarry
car park, Bleasdale, PR3
1UN (nearby), SD544457

DISTANCE 6½ miles (10.5km)

SUMMARY Easy

MAP OS Explorer OL41
Forest of Bowland

An easy walk around the Bleasdale estate on the south-west edge of the
Bowland Fells.

① From the car park turn left onto Delph Lane and walk 600yds,
with fields to the left and a fringe of woodland to the right.

② Just before a slight left-hand bend, take a footpath on the right
that cuts through the trees to place you on a tarmac road. Bear right.
Continue for 1 mile, passing Fell End Farm and Bleasdale Tower to
reach a junction by Brooks Barn.

③ Here, turn left and continue to Hazelhurst Farm. By this stage,
tarmac has given way to a broad farm track. After passing the large
complex of Hazelhurst, the track swings right and then left to pass
through the farm of Holme House.

④ On the far side of the farm keep on the track, now becoming
grassier as it turns southwards to cross the open marshy ground.
Ignore a footpath leading off to Higher Fairsnape on the left and
keep ahead. After a wooden gate, the track joins a farm lane close to
Admarsh Barn Farm on the right. Close by Vicarage Farm there is
an interesting diversion to be made to Bleasdale Circle. Turn left at
a signpost to take a concessionary path over pasture to an enclosed
plantation of conifers. After viewing Bleasdale Circle, return to the
farm road, turn left and keep ahead to St Eadmer's Church on the left
and Bleasdale Primary School on the right.

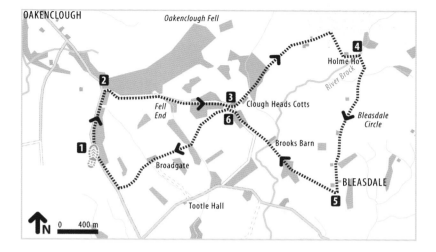

(5) At the junction after the primary school, turn right. The estate road leads back to Brooks Barn, which is reached in just less than a mile. Look out for the ancient packhorse bridge to the right of the road in half a mile.

(6) At Brooks Barn junction bear left onto a grassy track, which after a metal gate crosses a large field with a good view of Bleasdale Tower on your right. On reaching the next field, cross it diagonally left to a gate on its far side. Pass through a neck of woodland on a (muddy) track that leads to Broadgate Farm. Follow the signs to the left through its yard and then turn right. The footpath crosses to a stile and then continues up a slight rise, edging past a farm on the left. Following the hedge on the left will bring you to the farm's drive. This leads down to Delph Lane. Turn right for the car park.

Points of interest

Bleasdale was the site of a Bronze Age circle – so-called 'Woodhenge' – because it was constructed from timber posts. A set of small concrete posts mark the position of the inner circle.

START Freckleton village centre, PR4
1AA, SD429290. Given the linear
nature of the walk, it is necessary
to use public transport. There is
a regular bus service between
Preston and Blackpool (No. 68)
that passes through the village

DISTANCE 6½ miles (10.5km)

SUMMARY Easy

MAP OS Explorer 286
Blackpool & Preston

WHERE TO EAT AND DRINK
The route passes behind the Ship
(www.theshipinnfreckleton.co.uk),
and there are several pubs,
restaurants and cafés in Lytham

A walk along the first section of the Lancashire Coastal Way.

1   Standing before Holy Trinity Church on Lytham Rd, turn left
and then right onto Trinity Close. Follow this to its junction with
Preston Old Rd. Turn right. After 500yds where the road bends left,
keep ahead on a cobbled lane leading down to Freckleton Pool. Turn
right onto a footpath, which leads through Freckleton Dock. Now
on the Lancashire Coastal Way, shortly after the path divides at a
house. Follow waymark arrows to the right and then keep ahead with
the creek to the left. The scene opens out. Some 15mins after joining
it, the path turns right and then left around two properties before
entering a large field. In the far left corner stands a trig point.

2   The way drops down an embankment and turns right. Ahead,
acting as a guide post, is a large hangar, part of British Aerospace's
facility at Warton Aerodrome. This part of the coastal path couldn't
be called attractive in anyone's book, but the area is designated as a
National Nature Reserve for birdlife. About 15mins after joining the
Ribble you reach the perimeter fence of the aerodrome. For the next
1,000yds or so this acts as a useful handrail as the path winds its way
through hawthorn. When the mesh fence turns away distinctly to the
right, keep ahead across a meadow, following the frequent waymark
signs. The path leads to a lane below Warton Bank and a caravan park.
The lane leads out onto an embankment, which bears round to the
right to reach the A584.

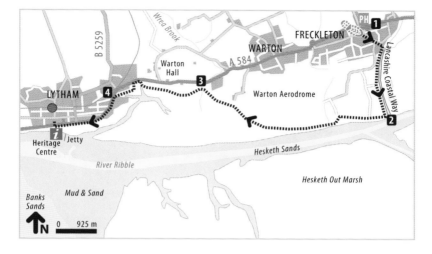

③ On reaching the road turn left, cross the bridge and turn immediately left onto a footpath that leads once more onto an embankment. With farmland on your right and marshland on your left, keep on the embankment until it brings you once more to the A584 and the very edge of Lytham itself. The Coastal Way turns left through Lytham Dock and its large boat repair yard. Once past the boatyard, follow a creek that once more and finally brings you to the A584.

④ Turn left and in 10mins you will reach the Green at Lytham with its most notable landmark – the handsome windmill.

Note: Buses to return to Freckleton leave from Clifton St, Lytham's main shopping area, which runs parallel to the front a few streets to its right.

Points of interest

Freckleton, a lively bustling place today, was the scene of terrible tragedy during World War Two. On 23 August 1944 an American bomber crashed into the village school, killing two teachers and thirty-eight children. In addition, another twenty-one civilians and servicemen died in the catastrophe. Behind the church there is a memorial to the victims of the crash.

Hesketh Bank

START Chapel Rd, Hesketh
Bank, PR4 6SA, SD437237

DISTANCE 6½ miles (10.5km)

SUMMARY Very flat, easy walking

MAP OS Explorer 286
Blackpool & Preston

WHERE TO EAT AND DRINK
Not on the route but nearby. Booths
supermarket on Station Rd has a
café open during shop hours; turn
left when you reach Station Rd

A walk of straight lines and sharp angles.

1   Walk to the junction of Chapel Rd with Shore Rd. On the
opposite side of Shore Rd take the footpath just to the left of a bus
stop. This leads out onto the flat landscape of Hesketh Old Marsh.
Here, farming is arable, taking advantage of the rich soil. After 700yds
(10mins) the track crosses a pronounced ditch. This is the Carr Heys
Watercourse. Here, turn left.

2   With the ditch on your left, walk for 800yds until you arrive at a
farm drive (Dib Rd). Turn right. Walk for a further 800yds to reach
Hesketh Lodge. Keep ahead for a further 400yds to reach the car
park of the RSPB Reserve Hesketh Out Marsh (see box). The way is
right but it is well worth having a look at the observation point about
200yds to the left, surmounting the embankment.

3   Returning to the car park, keep ahead on a gravel path with
a fence to the left. Through a gate, continue to the top of the
embankment. This will take you in a perfectly straight line to the
confluence of the Douglas and the Ribble. Although just a few feet
above sea level, there are extensive views. Across the river lies Warton
aerodrome, and ahead the skyline of Preston with the Bowland Fells as
a backdrop can easily be seen in clear weather.

4   The embankment turns right to follow the course of the River
Douglas. You are on it for another 2 miles – almost an hour. After

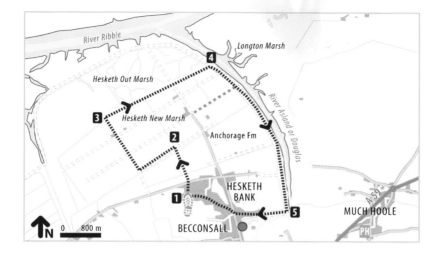

passing the sewage works on the right, walk for another 500yds and the embankment will turn sharply to the right. Immediately a boatyard will come into view. The path takes you through it.

⑤ On reaching the public footpath signpost at the entrance to the yard, turn right onto a lane that soon leads past an ancient brick-built chapel and its burial ground. Here, follow the lane as it turns left. As if stepping through some magic portal, you have now been returned to the familiar world of brick and tarmac. These quiet residential streets seem a world away from the marshes you have just walked across. After 500yds you will reach Station Rd. Turn right and then left into Chapel Rd.

Points of interest

Hesketh Out Marsh RSPB Reserve is an example of what conservationists call 'managed realignment'. With the threats posed by climate change and rising sea levels, flood wall defences have been constructed in many places along the coast, resulting in a loss of habitat for wildlife. At Hesketh Bank the seawater has been allowed to flood some of the land, creating a salt marsh reserve to compensate for losses elsewhere. The Ribble estuary is an internationally recognized area for sea birds and waders and attracts large numbers of resident and migrating species.

START Langden Intake, BB7
3BH (nearby), SD632512

DISTANCE 6½ miles (10.5km)

SUMMARY For the most part,
though the country is wild, the
walking uses shooters' tracks,
allowing good progress to be made

up and down the valleys. However,
at the top of Hareden Fell an
awkward moorland crossing has
to be made, which would prove
more difficult in misty conditions

MAP OS Explorer OL41
Forest of Bowland

This exceptional walk scales Hareden Fell and then crosses to Langden Castle,
before returning to the Trough of Bowland.

① From the road take the service road towards the intake, but
almost immediately turn left through a kissing gate and then cross
Langden Brook by way of a footbridge. The footpath beyond leads
alongside Langden Brook to Hareden. Close to Hareden cross a stile
on the right. After a footbridge turn right over a stile onto a farm road.

② As you reach the farmhouse beyond kennels, bear left over
a bridge and through a metal gate. Continue on the lane, quickly
reaching Hareden House and the water works of Hareden Intake.
Keep ahead to a gate and then, after a footbridge, continue along a
shooters' track which will take you to the top of Hareden Fell. As the
track levels out 1½ miles after the intake, you'll pass a shooting hut to
the right of the track. The track ends in a large turning circle close to
grouse butts.

③ Now comes the tricky bit – a 15min traverse of peat and heather
without a discernible path. The way is right of the turning circle,
slightly north of east. By keeping to the left of a small stream that
soon appears, you will intercept a ribbon of a path leading down
towards Bleadale Water. Gradually the path becomes more definite as
it descends into the valley. When you reach the valley bottom, turn
right. As you near the junction of valleys with Langden Castle – the

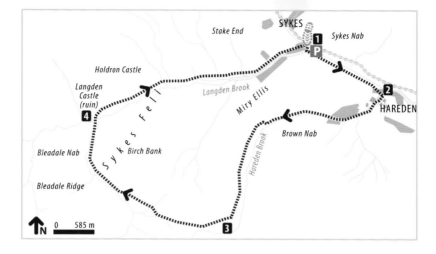

only building in sight – drop to a wooden gate and, after passing through it, aim for another. In between you will have to cross Bleadale Water. After the second gate you will have to cross Langden Brook. Aim well to the left of Langden Castle as you negotiate the streams. At some times of the year it will not be possible to do this without getting your feet wet.

④ Close inspection of Langden Castle reveals that it is not a castle at all – it's a shooting lodge. When you reach it, turn right onto a track, following Langden Brook downstream until you arrive back at the car park.

Points of interest

United Utilities owns 26,000 acres of land in the Forest of Bowland Area of Outstanding Natural Beauty. Its presence is much in evidence at Langden and Hareden, with intakes that help manage the collection of water. In winter when there is less foliage, it may be possible to see 'Miranda', a statue of a naked nymph on one of the pools at the Langden Intake, put there to commemorate the completion of works in 1954.

WALK

77   **Crown Point** ➤

START Crown Point picnic
area, on Crown Point Rd, BB11
5SN (nearby), SD848288

DISTANCE 7 miles (11.3km)

SUMMARY Moderate

MAP OS Explorer OL21
South Pennines

A wide circuit of Clowbridge Reservoir, with wonderful moorland views.

① From the car park turn left and take a footpath to the right of a
cattle grid. To begin with, this keeps roughly parallel to the road. Soon
it is passing through a plantation of trees. When the track divides, fork
right. In a little over 300yds the path reaches a junction. Here, turn
right. On a more substantial track continue to the next wall. At this
point you will join the Rossendale Way, which comes in from your
left, close to a restored stone cross. Here, keep ahead along a broad,
peaty track, passing below pylons. Stay on this track for 900yds, with a
wall on your left.

② As the way reaches the top of a rise, approximately 750yds from
the pylons, near a stone squeeze stile in a wall on the left, take a faint
track on the right leading downhill towards Clowbridge Reservoir. As
you near the reservoir, you will intercept a more definite track. Here,
turn left. Once on it, keep on it until you reach Manchester Rd. Turn
left and immediately enter the village of Dunnockshaw.

③ Cross Manchester Rd and after 200yds take a footpath on the
right. This leads across a field to the edge of a farm complex. The
route goes through the gate, crosses the yard and then bears right
to cross a footbridge. Enter the woodland on a marked arrow path,
cross a second stream and head in a northerly direction to the edge

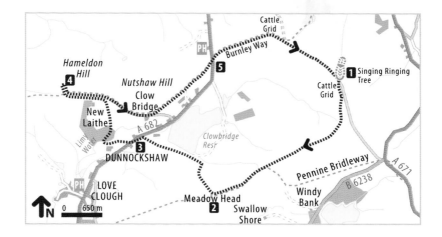

of the wood. From here, follow a grassy track to reach a service road 200yds east of New Laithe Farm. Turn left. As the road bends to the left, continue straight through two boulders onto a stony track. This track is reunited with the road 300yds ahead. On reaching the edge of the summit plateau, turn right in front of the wall to reach the radar weather station. The trig point is to its left across a broken wall. The views are extensive.

④ Return to the service road and the point where you joined it. Here, keep ahead. You are now on the Burnley Way and will stay on it almost all the way back to Crown Point. After 700yds branch left off the service road to take a track leading behind cottages. The way maintains a parallel course to the busy A682 for over 1,000yds, before crossing it to the south of the New Waggoners public house.

⑤ The way soon climbs into rough moorland. Great views open out, with Pendle prominent to the north. Keep on the way until you reach Crown Point Rd. Turn right. After 600yds take a footpath on the left that keeps close to the road, leading you back to the car park. A short extension to the walk will bring you to the Singing Ringing Tree – Burnley's panopticon – and a wonderful climax to the walk.

START The youth hostel in Earby,
BB18 6JX, SD915469 (roadside parking
unless you are staying at the hostel)

DISTANCE 7 miles (11.3km)

SUMMARY Moderate

MAP OS Explorer OL21
South Pennines

After the 1974 local government reorganization, this area of the Craven District
was one of Lancashire's gains. This circuit in the disputed borderlands of east
Lancashire will show what a delightful gain it is.

① From Birch Hall Lane follow the sign towards the hostel car park.
Before you reach it, go through a gap in the low wall on the left and
follow a path down to a footbridge over Wentcliffe Brook and up steps
on the far side. After a gate cross a pasture to one on the far side. Cross
a farm track and continue with the field boundary on your left. At the
next farm road turn right towards Batty House, but before you reach
it cross a stile on the left. Follow the fence through a wooden gate and
keep ahead to a field corner. Cross the corner using two stiles and
cross the next field, passing by a stone squeeze stile in a ditch. Aiming
for the left corner of the next field, drop down and cross a stile onto a
farm road. Turn left. This leads across Earby Beck at Booth Bridge and
continues for ¾ mile to arrive at the attractive village of Thornton-in-
Craven.

② Cross the A56 directly into Stockbridge Lane. This quickly leaves
the village and, after passing through the farm complex at Shed Laithe
in 400yds, continues along a hedged lane. When the track reaches
open country, go through a metal gate. Cross a large field to a stone
footbridge and stile. After this, cross Castleber Hill to a gate leading
onto the Leeds–Liverpool Canal. Keep ahead, with the water on
your right.

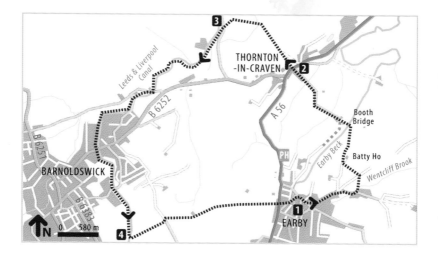

3. Put away these directions for the next hour as the towpath crosses to the right side, climbs through Greenberfield Locks to the summit level, passes through Barnoldswick and then at Bridge 153 (close to the Silent Night factory) switches back to the left side. Carry on for 700yds to Cockshott Bridge.

4. Here, the Pendle Way turns right over the bridge. Turn left through a wooden gate and follow a well-defined track over a rise and across two large fields to reach a gate leading to a lane. Briefly on the Pennine Bridleway, turn left and then immediately right towards Kayfield Farm. At the farm keep ahead on a grassy track that skirts it to its right. Cross a stile next to a metal gate and then, bearing left, cross to a gate at a corner. Through this, keep ahead to another stile/metal gate combo (beneath telephone wires). Cross the next huge field, aiming for a tall metal stack which can be seen in Earby. This will put you in line with a stile leading into a sunken lane. Follow this as it leads into Earby. Cross the A56 into Albion Rd. Turn right onto Victoria Rd. Turn left and from here follow signs for the youth hostel.

Glasson Dock

Start Car park at Glasson Dock, by the marina, LA2 0AW, SD445560

Distance 7 miles (11.3km)

Summary Flat, easy walking

Map OS Explorer 296 Lancaster, Morecambe & Fleetwood

An easy walk by the Lune estuary, visiting the ruins of Cockersand Abbey.

①   From the car park walk into the village, crossing the bridge between the marina and dock. Continue along Tithe Barn Hill to a junction with a fine viewpoint across the Lune estuary. A signpost will confirm you are on the Lancashire Coastal Way. Turn left and after 300yds turn right into Marsh Lane. After 400yds Marsh Lane passes into pasture land to follow a track to Crook Farm. At Crook Farm turn left on a tarmac drive with the estuary on your right. Beyond Abbey Lighthouse Cottage you will reach the car park for visitors to Cockersand Abbey. From this point the way reverts to a footpath. The route is obvious and the chapter house of the abbey can be seen from some distance. Indeed the chapter house is all that remains of the abbey.

②   Continue on the Coastal Way past the caravan park to arrive at Bank End and its caravan park. Beyond the farm complex you will find yourself once more on tarmac, with a raised embankment on your left. After 800yds the lane turns sharply left (where the Coastal Way continues to Patty's Farm).

③   Follow the lane as it climbs up to the hamlet of Hillam. By Hillam Farm turn left onto a footpath, which will take you through the farm and across pastures to the white farmhouse of Norbreck Farm. Although only 60ft above sea level, this elevation provides an almost

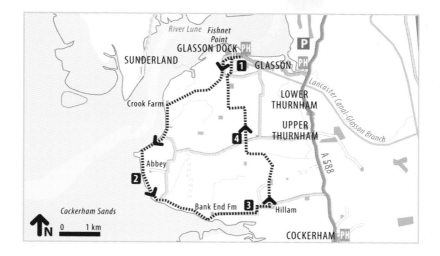

unexpected viewing platform for the countryside around. At Norbreck
Farm turn right and follow waymarkers through the yard to reach a
rough track. Ahead, a trig point will be seen. The track descends the
ridge to the right of this and then swings into the next field. From
the gate bear slightly left, crossing the field to reach the end of a
drainage ditch and a metal gate. Go through the gate and turn right.
In the corner of the field cross a stile and turn left. Keep the hedge on
your left as you traverse three fields (350yds/5mins). When you see a
footbridge on the left, turn right. With a tall hedgerow on your right,
keep ahead until you reach Moss Lane.

4 Cross the lane obliquely right to metal gates. Go through both.
After 400yds pass a derelict building on the left. Take a stile on the left
and go immediately right. Keep ahead for almost 300yds and then, at a
fence, turn left. Follow a grassy track for a little under 300yds and then
turn right. This is Dobs Lane and soon you will pass the twin towers
of Old Glasson. At the road junction turn right into School Lane.
Walk down to the school and follow the sign for its entrance. This will
quickly put you on a narrow path on the edge of the marina. Keep left
and on reaching a children's playground turn left into the village.

Parbold

START Parbold village hall car
park, WN8 7DN, SD491108

DISTANCE 7 miles (11.3km)

SUMMARY A mainly easy walk,
with a moderate amount of effort
required to ascend Fairy Glen

MAP OS Explorer 285
Southport & Chorley

This walk begins in the village below Parbold Hill and will take you to the highest
point via Fairy Glen, before returning by way of High Moor and Harrock Hill.

① From the car park walk back to the parade of shops, turning
left into Tann House Lane. At the next T-junction turn right
into Lancaster Lane. On meeting the A5209, turn right and then
immediately left into Wood Lane. A stone sign marks the end of the
metalled lane to put you on a farm track. On reaching a large house,
pass through a pair of kissing gates onto a public footpath. On a well
waymarked trail you will pass through patches of woodland and cross
pastureland to reach a stile leading into Fairy Glen.

② Cross and bear left to follow a footpath beside Sprodley Brook
through woodland up to the A5209. On leaving the wood, turn right.
Cross the road and, after 200yds near the far end of a lay-by, turn left
onto a track. In 100yds the path divides. Bear right towards Boar's Den
Farm. Passing the farm, turn left onto a track. This leads onto a path,
which 500yds (7½mins) from the farm will bring you onto High Moor
Lane. Turn left on reaching the lane. After 100yds turn right onto a
drive just before High Moor Restaurant. After 500yds, when the drive
swings left down to Harrock Hall, bear right on a gently ascending
footpath. After passing through a patch of woodland, turn right onto
a track leading upwards beside the mesh fence of a covered reservoir.
Ahead is a tall radio mast. Close by, though sadly not accessible since
it is on the other side of the mesh fence, is the triangulation column –
the highest point of the walk at 157m (515ft in old money).

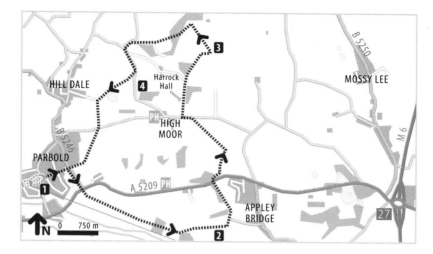

③ Retrace your steps to the patch of woodland to pick up a path leading to a stile. Continue on a clear path with a fence on your right and, at the next plantation, dog-leg right around the wood to reach the ruins of the old windmill that marks the top of Harrock Hill. At the mill turn left onto a footpath that leads down through gorse towards a cluster of converted farm buildings. The right of way follows a drive to the right down to Jackson's Lane. Turn left onto Jackson's Lane, which after a double bend will bring you onto Bannister Lane. Turn left and begin to climb steeply again.

④ Near the top of the brow turn right onto a footpath below Hunter's Hill Quarry. When the path meets a track, turn right then left onto a footpath that crosses two fields to bring you onto Stony Lane. Turn right, then in 100yds turn left onto a footpath. The path soon begins a gentle descent to Parbold. After crossing a stile, continue until you reach a footbridge which puts you in the adjoining field on the left. Follow the path as it skirts the field to enter a lane that brings you onto Lancaster Lane, close to the primary school. Tann House Lane opposite will take you back to the village centre.

Start Shore Rd, close to Red
Bank Farm caravan site, Bolton-
le-Sands, LA5 8JR, SD472682

Distance 7½ miles (12km)

Summary Easy. NB: Follow all
advice concerning tides displayed
on noticeboards at start of walk

Maps OS Explorer 296 Lancaster,
Morecambe & Fleetwood, and
OS Explorer OL7 The English
Lakes, South-eastern area

Where to eat and drink There
are numerous eateries in Carnforth
if the nostalgia of the Refreshment
Room, www.therefreshmentroom.com,
T01524-732432, is not to your taste

This route could not be easier. From Bolton-le-Sands it follows the Lancashire
Coastal Way to Carnforth and returns along the Lancaster Canal. It is a walk full
of interest, though – not least the railway station at Carnforth, where Trevor met
Celia briefly in 1945.

① With Morecambe Bay on your left, walk along the raised
embankment northwards. After St Michael's Lane the embankment
ends, so continue on the flat reaching Wild Duck Hall, a large
white building. Keep to the left of the hall on a service road leading
to Bolton Holmes Farm. From this point, the way is a little less
straightforward in that the salt marshes are dissected by creeks and
pools which need to be carefully negotiated, especially when the tide
is high. After a rock-strewn point of land, the way reaches the estuary
of the River Keer close to Marsh House Farm. After a stile, continue
along the lane which brings you to the junction where the Coastal
Way turns left. Here, keep ahead on Crag Bank Lane, passing beneath
a pair of railway bridges to a road junction. Turn right for Carnforth.

② The route continues past the station to the busy road junction
with the A6. Cross the road at traffic lights and continue slightly
uphill to the canal bridge. Just before it turn right and, following the
access path around a children's playground, reach the towpath. With
the canal on your left, walk back to Bolton-le-Sands. This is easy,
uncomplicated walking.

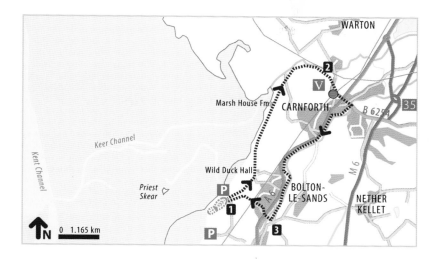

③ About an hour (2½ miles) will bring you back to Bolton-le-Sands. Pass under Church Bridge (No. 122) and then take the path up to St Michael's Lane. Turn left and, soon after, cross the A6. Still on St Michael's Lane, continue through a housing estate and cross the railway by a level crossing. The lane then quickly returns you to the shore and car park.

Points of interest

Carnforth railway station was one of the locations of the 1945 British film classic Brief Encounter, starring Celia Johnson and Trevor Howard. In fact the plot centres on a relationship that starts, develops and ends in the station refreshment room. Because of this, Carnforth attracts thousands of visitors every year to soak up the atmosphere. Today, you can re-enact your favourite scenes in the Refreshment Room, which retains the look and ambience of the late 1940s, or else immerse yourself in the exhibits of the adjacent visitors' centre.

START Dunsop Bridge car park (pay
& display), BB7 3BB, SD661501

DISTANCE 7½ miles (12km)

SUMMARY Moderate.
Note: This route uses stepping
stones over the Hodder near the
Inn at Whitewell and should only be
attempted when the river level is low

A lovely circuit in the Hodder Valley.

1 Walk back towards the bridge and turn right onto a tarmac track
just past Puddleducks Café. Follow this as it leads across fields to reach
a row of cottages. Keep ahead on a path leading into woods and then
cross the river by a wooden footbridge. Turn left. After 200yds turn
right before farm buildings and cross pasture. In 500yds you will reach
the Trough of Bowland Rd. Turn right. In 800yds turn left to cross a
bridge and enter the hamlet of Hareden.

2 Keep on the service road through the hamlet. Cross Hareden
Brook (again) on a flat bridge, turning right. Almost immediately
cross a short ladder stile onto a bridleway. This is the start of a steep
climb towards Mellor Knoll. After the next stile a large pasture opens
out. Look for a marker post and head up in a south-easterly direction.
As you near the top of a col, cross a ladder stile and, as the ground
levels off, bear right to reach a wall crossed by yet another ladder
stile. As the way begins to gently drop, bear left to follow a wall/
fence that will bring you to a scattered wood. On a more definite
track pass through a gate and keep ahead. The track dips to a brook
and then climbs up briefly to enter a conifer plantation. After 500yds
pass through a gate into pasture and follow the track until it reaches a
farm road. Turn left. Keep on the farm road as it bears first to the left
past a junction and then to the right. Past a house with a distinctive
conservatory, turn left onto an unmarked right of way. Cross the
pasture in the direction of a quarry to reach a lane via a stile.

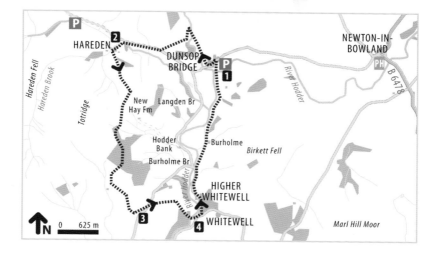

[3] Cross the lane, go through a gate and follow the direction of the finger post past a quarry and down the hill. After a gate keep the fence on the right. Go through another gate and continue downhill. The footpath reaches a farm lane close by a cheese press. Turn right, pass through New Laund Farm and after a gate continue downhill to the River Hodder, keeping the wall on your right. Cross the stepping stones over the river. Once across, turn left along a riverside path to reach the rear of the famous inn.

[4] Pass the front of the inn at Whitewell and turn left and locate the concessionary path on the left of the road (this will necessitate shimmying over the roadside wall). After a wooded section, the path crosses a footbridge into meadows. Keep to the fence until a stile is reached that puts you onto the road. Before you reach Burholme Bridge, take the track on the right leading to Burholme. Pass through the farm and cross a brook by a footbridge. Keep ahead, crossing fields and stiles. Ignore the metal pipe bridge and cross the Hodder at Thorneyholme Hall. Turn left at the end of its drive for the car park.

START Lay-by in Crown Point
Rd just before its junction
with the A671 Burnley–Bacup
Rd, BB11 3RT, SD852278

DISTANCE 7½ miles (12km)

SUMMARY Moderate

MAP OS Explorer OL21
South Pennines

WHERE TO EAT AND DRINK
The Hargreaves Arms, to the right
as you reach Lumb,
http://thehargreavesarms.co.uk,
T01706-215523

A superb moorland walk, mainly in Rossendale.

① From the lay-by cross the road to a track leading south-west
into the barrenness of moorland. On a broad, gravelly track keep
ahead for ¾ mile to reach a junction close by pylons and a feature
known as Compton's Cross. At this point you join the Rossendale
Way. From the cross keep ahead on a grassy track with a wall to the
left. Down to the right views open up of Clowbridge Reservoir. The
path is well waymarked and in 1½ miles brings you above relatively
new development close to Love Clough. On reaching Swinshaw Lane,
turn left.

② Pass the chapel on the left and then turn left onto a farm drive to
enter a field and bear right on a footpath to a wooded corner. After a
kissing gate follow the path to a squeeze stile and then cross a track
to an enclosed path. When this reaches a broad track, turn left into a
wooded valley, once the site of a textile mill. Following the path into
the valley, which becomes progressively steep-sided, the old water
workings will be seen. Beyond a small footbridge the path switches
to the right of the stream. Climb out of the valley assisted by a flight
of concrete steps and then follow a fence on the right to a wooden
kissing gate. Here, turn right to pass a large barn on the left. On
reaching the farm drive, turn left and cross a wooden stile.

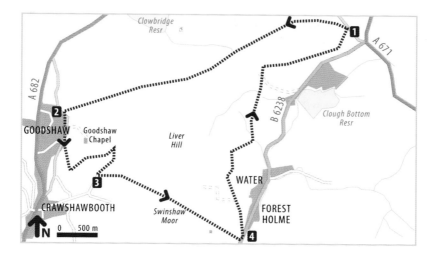

3   With the fence on your left, keep ahead in a large field for 200yds and then bear right to a wooden stile next to a hooped metal gate. From here the route continues in a straight line, following field boundaries for 400yds. At a stile with a waymark pointing diagonally left, cross the wall on the right and continue through very rough pasture to cross a stile in a fence. Keep ahead in the next field to reach a grassy track leading to metal gates. Through these, turn right passing a farmhouse on the right and join its main drive down to Lumb.

4   On reaching Burnley Rd, turn left and then almost immediately turn left again onto Peers Clough Rd. At this point you have joined the Pennine Bridleway, which leads nearly all the way back to the car park. The road leads onto a broad farm track. After passing the entrance to Peersclough Farm, the way swings right and then in a further 300yds at a junction of paths bears right again, following a hedge to a wooden gate. Keep ahead as the way dips below Far Pastures and then climbs up towards the pylons, passed earlier on the outward leg. Turn right on the Pennine Bridleway as you reach a junction close to a wall, and then before reaching Burnley Rd turn left onto a track that leads back to the car park.

Mawdesley Jubilee Trail ▶

START Car park opposite the village
hall, Mawdesley, L40 2QT, SD492150

DISTANCE 7½ miles (12km)

SUMMARY Mainly flat and easy

MAP OS Explorer 285
Southport & Chorley

USEFUL WEBSITE
www.mawdesley-village.org.uk

A dedicated trail following the boundaries of the attractive west Lancashire
village.

① From the car park walk ahead into the Millennium Green and
follow the path as it swings round to the left. Over a footbridge turn
right on a footpath that will bring you onto Smithy Lane. Turn right
and walk down to the junction with Sandy Lane. Turn left, and then
after 150yds turn left onto a footpath. Keep on this path for 500yds to
reach High St, close to St Peter's Church. Take the footpath beside the
churchyard and follow it as it curves to the right to reach School Lane.
Here, turn left and bear left at the junction, reaching Cedar Farm
Galleries.

② Take the footpath passing to the right of the Galleries. The
footpath turns left behind the complex and continues to a farm track.
At the track turn left. When the track reaches Back Lane, turn right.
Almost immediately the lane bends to the left. Just after the bend, turn
right onto a footpath. Keep ahead with the field boundary on your
left. When the hedge ends, cross the field to Moody Lane. Turn left
and then immediately take the right fork. After passing House Farm
on the right, turn left onto a drive. Keep ahead through the yard of
the house to the right. The path skirts a large meadow, bringing you
to a footbridge. Keep ahead to reach Bradshaw Brow. Cross the lane
and keep ahead across pasture to arrive at Tarnbrook Dr. Turn right.
As the drive swings to the left, turn right to cross a footbridge. With a
hedge on your right, follow the edge of the field around to the left. At
the bottom turn right to reach the entrance of an old quarry on Hall
Lane. Turn right.

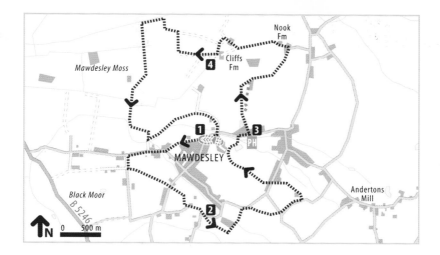

[3] At the Black Bull turn left. Keep ahead at a gate to follow a track into a large field. Here, follow a track which bends to the right, which will lead you to a stile at the corner of a wood. Cross the next field to a footbridge. Beyond the footbridge keep ahead, with the field boundary on your right. The path passes a large property to reach Wood Lane. Turn left. At the next junction bear right and after the first farm turn left to reach the activity centre.

[4] At the centre turn right onto a track leading out to Mawdesley Moss. At a junction of tracks turn right. After 250yds turn left along a hedge. As this comes to an end, turn right, crossing an arable field towards an isolated hawthorn tree. At the field edge turn left. At the next junction turn left onto a more obvious track. With wind turbines to your left, cross the Moss to Gales Lane. Follow the lane for 800yds. Just before a bridge turn left onto a footpath, which follows a brook on your right. This leads to a tree-lined lane. Walk up this to Hall Lane, not far from the village centre. Turn right for the car park.

START National Trust car park at Eaves Wood, Park Rd, Silverdale, LA5 0UG (nearby), SD759472

DISTANCE 7½ miles (12km)

SUMMARY Mainly easy walking, with a modest climb to the Pepperpot (optional)

MAP OS Explorer OL7 The English Lakes, South-eastern area

A circular walk taking in a pleasant village, woodlands, pastureland, seashore and inland waters.

1️⃣ From the car park take a track 200yds north. Turn left at the signpost marked 'The Cove' and follow the path for about ½ mile along the edge of woodland. (After 500yds you can follow the signposts to the Pepperpot for a great view. This will add about 40mins to your walk.) As you leave the woods, turn left, following the signposted track to the Cove. Walk through Elmslack down to the road and in 100yds fork left onto Cove Rd and keep ahead to reach the Cove.

2️⃣ From the Cove take a footpath on the left that leads across pastures, known as 'The Lotts', to reach Shore Rd. Turn left. At Stankelt Rd turn left again and then left into the village centre. After the fire station turn right onto St John's Grove and continue onto Churchfield. Continue straight on a path for 'Bottoms Lane'. Turn right on the road and after 50yds take a path left over fields to 'The Row'. Turn right on The Row and after 300yds take the second footpath on the left signed 'The Railway'. This crosses the golf course to Red Bridge Lane. Turn right, pass the railway station, then turn left onto Storrs Lane.

3️⃣ Almost immediately on the right you will pass the RSPB visitor centre for the nationally important Leighton Moss Wildlife Reserve. Continue along the lane for 350yds and then turn right onto a broad track that leads across the wetlands of Leighton Moss. At the far side pass through a gate and take the track leading past a barn to reach

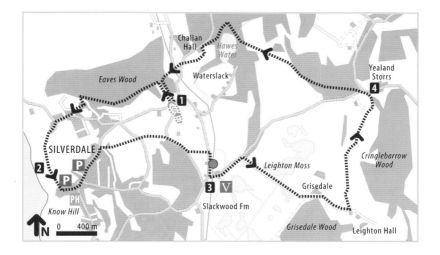

Griesdale Farm. Keep ahead on the farm road for 450yds and, just before you reach Keeper's Cottage and Home Farm, turn left onto a footpath. This leads north across several fields to Yealand Storrs. After the first gate the hedge is on your right. Maintain the northward direction and after 500yds take the right gate, with the wall now to your left.

④ On reaching the village, turn left. Walk down to where the road forks. Take the footpath going straight ahead, signposted 'Hawes Water'. Follow the track for 800yds through woodland and then along the edge of fields. As the track begins to descend, go through a squeeze stile next to a metal gate. Continue diagonally right across the meadow to reach a stile through a wall into Gait Barrows Nature Reserve. Cross a meadow, and follow the path down to a kissing gate to enter the woods near Hawes Water. Turn right onto a wooden walkway. Keep on the footpath round Hawes Water to its junction with a bridleway, then turn left. Take the permissive footpath over fields on the left. Turn right 100yds after Challan Hall. Cross over the road and follow the signpost 'Waterslack and Eaves Wood'. In 100yds, on reaching a lane, turn left then right on a footpath that crosses the railway. Keep ahead on a path that crosses a service road into Eaves Wood. Keep ahead on the track until it reaches the junction leading left to the car park.

START Slaidburn village, pay &
display car park, BB7 3ES, SD714523

DISTANCE 7½ miles (12km)

SUMMARY Moderate

MAP OS Explorer OL41
Forest of Bowland

WHERE TO EAT AND DRINK
Hark to Bounty,
www.harktobounty.co.uk,
T01200-446246;
Riverbank Tearooms,
www.riverbanktearooms.co.uk,
T01200-446398

A varied walk with fine views.

1 From the car park turn right and then right again at the war
memorial. Cross Croasdale Bridge and turn right onto a footpath
leading across pastures for over 600yds to Holmehead Bridge. Cross
the bridge and follow the broad track up to Hammerton Hall. Just
past this, turn left onto a footpath taking you to the right of conifer
plantations over Ten Acre Hill. At Black House turn left onto a farm
drive leading to a lane corner.

2 Keep ahead and turn right onto a faint footpath about 250yds
from the corner. Follow the path through woodland to reach a stone
stile leading out to a pasture. Cross the field to a metal gate and a
rough track leading past an isolated barn. Keep on the track as it
leads to Brook House Green. At the farm drive, turn left to follow it to
Dugdale Lane. Turn right.

3 Keep on the lane as it crosses the B6478 and then climbs up
towards Holden. After 750yds the road bends to the left. Here, climb
over a ladder stile, taking the left of two footpaths. Ahead, aim
towards the left corner of an isolated building marked 'Champion' on
the map. To do this you will have to negotiate a large patch of marshy
ground to reach a stile to the right of a brook. Over this, follow the
brook to a culvert on the left and then continue to a wooden gate close

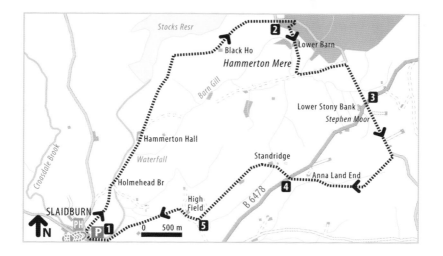

to the building. Pass the building and then bear right across pastures on a path leading over stiles, aiming for the farmhouse of Anna Land End. The path passes below the property and then climbs up to the B6478.

④ Cross the road directly and then descend towards a large farm. As you approach it, follow the footpath on the left. This follows a fence on the left up to a tall kissing gate. Turn left through this and continue with the hedge on the right. The path climbs up to Pikefield Plantation and then drops towards Higher High Field Farm.

⑤ The path follows a fence on the left, before bearing right to a wall beyond a farm track. Cross the wall and turn left and then in the corner of the field drop to a stile, cross a plank bridge and turn right onto a drive. Pass Lower High Field farmhouse and then turn left onto a path that leads through a narrow pasture to more open fields. Cross a brook on the left and then follow the wall as it leads to a broad sloping meadow. Cross to a footbridge hidden in a depression and then cross the wall above it to continue diagonally right, descending towards the Hodder. Go through a wooden kissing gate and keep ahead to reach the bridge over the river, close to Slaidburn. Turn right for the village.

START Brierfield railway
station, BB9 5PU, SD845365

DISTANCE 8 miles (13km)

SUMMARY Moderate

MAP OS Explorer OL21
South Pennines

A delightful exploration of the parish of Old Laund.

[1] From the railway station head downhill, and where the road forks just before the bridge bear right to reach a footpath to the left. Go under the motorway and then cross Quaker Bridge. Turn right onto a lane. In 250yds take the left fork uphill. After Old Laund Hall continue uphill through one gate, turning left at a second gate. Follow the path across fields to the A6068. Cross the road and then take a narrow path to cottages, turning right at a stile. Keep ahead on a back lane to reach Wheatley Lane and the Inghamite Church.

[2] Turn right on Wheatley Lane. At the Sparrowhawk Inn turn left onto a footpath at the rear. Climb to the far right corner of a pasture. After a stone stile bear left and almost immediately cross a step stile over the wall. Aim for the wall corner ahead. Follow the wall up to Noggarth Lane. Go straight across to a footpath. Turn left at a wall corner and cross to a stile. Over this, turn right onto a drive. After passing through the entrance of a farm, turn left, heading diagonally uphill to a wooded gully. The path continues towards Higher Spen Farm and its nearby telecom mast. As you near the farm, bear right behind it to a stile and cross a paddock diagonally right to a wooden gate. Turn left, bearing slightly right to a gate. Through this, follow the track to a farm and lane. Turn immediately left over a stile and cross a pasture. After a stile turn right on a farm track, returning you to the lane.

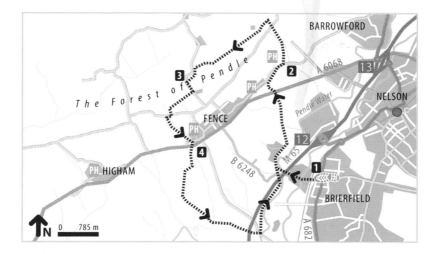

③ Turn left. At Height Cottages turn right onto a footpath that crosses pasture to a stone stile. Continue to a kissing gate close to a hedge. Keep ahead to a footbridge also on the left. Cross this and head downhill. When you reach the lane, turn right and then just beyond the houses turn left at a second footpath sign. At a corner drop to a stile leading to the adjoining field. Turn left and follow the path downhill to Fence.

④ Cross the car park of the Bay Horse to a stile. Cross the A6068 to a footpath opposite. This leads diagonally right to a gate. Turn left into the field. Keep ahead to a gate after a plank bridge. Turn right. After 150yds at a waymarked post bear diagonally left over the large field to a stile in its far corner. Continue in the same direction to a stile next to a gate. Over this and turn left on the farm road. This leads down to Wood End Farm. Before reaching it, turn left onto the Pendle Way. Follow this as it crosses fields to a footbridge over the M65. On the far side descend Pendle Bridge. Cross Greenhead Lane onto a tarmac track. Keep ahead to a metal gate and then turn right past a cottage on a riverside track, leading you back to Quaker Bridge.

88 Pilling

START Car park, Fluke Hall Lane, Pilling, PR3 6HP (nearby), SD389500

DISTANCE 8 miles (13km)

SUMMARY Flat and easy with one surprising ascent

MAP OS Explorer 296 Lancaster, Morecambe & Fleetwood

This walk will put you on an attractive stretch of the Lancashire Coastal Way, the long distance path that follows the coast between Merseyside and Cumbria.

① Walk back towards Fluke Hall and turn right onto a footpath just beyond the car park. Cross the field to a metal gate and keep ahead in the next field until an extensive ruin is reached. Here, waymark arrows will direct you slightly to the left past a small pond. Crossing a footbridge into the next field, keep the hedge on your left to reach a second bridge. After crossing it, turn right and walk down to the corner of the field to a stile. The footpath will bring you out by Beech House. At Beech House turn left and then at the T-junction turn right. This places you on Wheel Lane. Walk past the Springfield House Hotel and down to the T-junction. Here, turn right into Hooles Lane and follow it as it dog-legs to a slight bend in the road.

② Here, turn right into Ned's Lane, a farm track. Keep ahead until the next junction of tracks is reached. Turn right and, after soon passing cottages, reach another lane. Keep ahead to the next bend (200yds) and enter a large arable field. Cross on an obvious path to a gate in the hedge. Here, turn left and, again crossing an arable field, reach a stile close to some outbuildings. Keep ahead and after a second wooden kissing gate turn right towards Bourbles Farm. After passing the farm on the right, continue along a track that will quickly bring you to two fishing ponds. Before the second take a footpath on the left. Cross an obscure stile in the field boundary to the right of the pond. After a small footbridge maintain the same direction to reach a stile on the far side of the field. Then take a very overgrown path onto the end of a residential lane. Turn right and walk down to the B5270 Lancaster Rd.

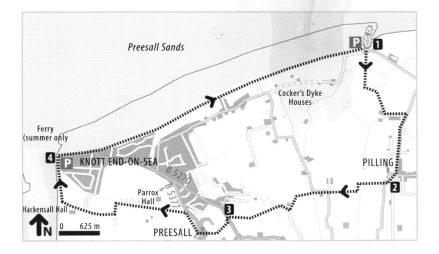

3 Turn left and then right onto a footpath across a field. Turn left
as you enter the next field and then after a stile bear right to scale
the heights of Preesall after a footbridge. Before the school turn right
onto a footpath that will bring you out on Mill Lane. Keep ahead and
descend to the main road (B5377). Here, turn right to walk through
the village past the Saracen's Head and the Black Bull. Beyond the
village cross a bridge and take a footpath on the left, which will put
you on the line of a disused railway. Keep straight ahead on the track
for almost 1,000yds and, at a point where it is about to enter a wooded
section, turn left onto a broad track (Whinney Lane). Follow this as it
takes you to the complex of Hackensall Hall on your left, where you
join the Wyre Way. Soon it crosses a fairway of Knott End Golf Club
to reach the promenade before Knott End Ferry.

4 After joining the Lancashire Coastal Way, at the approach to the
ferry, keep on it until you reach the car park back at Fluke Hall – a
distance of a little under 3 miles.

Stocks Reservoir

START Forest of Gisburn, School Lane car park, BB7 4TS (nearby), SD731566

DISTANCE 8 miles (13km)

SUMMARY Easy, with two pronounced gradients

MAP OS Explorer OL41 Forest of Bowland

WHERE TO EAT AND DRINK The Fishing Lodge offers light refreshments

A superb circuit in one of the most attractive parts of the county – if not the country.

① This route is waymarked all the way round the reservoir. Facing the reservoir, take the track leading from the right-hand corner of the car park. The first feature worth visiting is a birdwatchers' hide on the left of the path. Here you'll quickly come to appreciate the importance of Stocks as a nature site. From the hide continue along a broad track to reach a stone bridge over Hasgill Beck. The trail climbs steadily to the ruin of New House, which is reached 800yds after the beck.

② Before reaching the building, turn left on a broad track. The trail breaks out into open pasture and sweeps down to the River Hodder. After crossing the footbridge, the path continues over pasture to a kissing gate. Through it, turn right. For the next section of the walk you will be out of sight of the reservoir as you climb up alongside Copped Hill Clough and then turn left onto a broad track leading around Eak Hill.

③ This track provides excellent walking for the next 2 miles. The route gradually returns to the shore. As the track nears the dam, it reaches the fishing lodge and a complex of utility buildings. From the lodge the trail takes a service road, which passes through a 'Life for Life' memorial forest before reaching the drive of the imposing Stocks Board House. Here, the way leads onto the dam. This holds back 12 billion litres of water. At the far end there is a memorial plaque

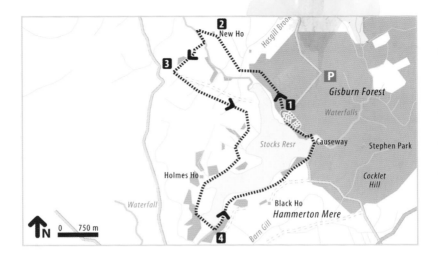

commemorating the opening of the reservoir in 1932. To the right of the dam take the service track to the end and turn left.

4. Keep ahead on a footpath, with the reservoir on your left. As you gain a little height you will have fine views across the water towards the Bowland Fells. After passing through a conifer plantation the trail leads down to the road. Turn left for the car park on a concessionary path parallel to it (though a right turn will take you to the chapel at Dalehead – a worthwhile diversion). After the causeway a path to the left will take you through shoreline woods back to the car park.

Points of interest

The ruins of the Church of St James are located close to the car park at the start of the walk. This was demolished by Fylde Waterboard and re-sited on higher ground at Dalehead. This building is still in use and also acts as an information point about wildlife and local history.

Towneley Park

START Riverside car park (pay
& display), Towneley Park,
Burnley, BB11 3RQ, SD856314

DISTANCE 8 miles (13km)

SUMMARY Undulating

MAP OS Explorer OL21
South Pennines

WHERE TO EAT AND DRINK
The Ram, www.theramburnley.co.uk,
To1282-459091; The Stables Café,
Towneley Hall, To1282-430111

A route connecting the lovely parkland of Towneley to the wild Pennine
moorlands.

1 From the car park cross the river by the nearby bridge and turn
left, with playing fields on the right. In 250yds follow the way as it
bears left across a wooden footbridge and begins to climb, at first
through woods then out onto broad pastures, taking you across to the
farm of Cliviger Laithe. A short way along its drive, bear left onto a
footpath that crosses a large field to Red Lees Rd. Cross the road and
continue on a path dropping gently downhill, bearing right towards a
metal kissing gate, and continue to a wooden kissing gate leading onto
Salterford Lane. Turn left.

2 After passing the Hurstwood village sign, cross the River Brun
and turn right onto a footpath that follows the valley bottom before
climbing up to Hurstwood, entering the village close to Hurstwood
Hall. Keep ahead until you reach Spencer's House and then turn
right onto a path, dropping once more to cross the River Brun, then
climbing to Foxstones Lane. Turn left.

3 From this point until you arrive at the wind farm on Warcock
Hill – the next 2 miles (almost an hour's walk) – keep on the Burnley
Way as it leads you through farms Crow Holes and Middle Pasture
and then drops to pass through the manmade landscape of Sheddon
Clough. Immediately beyond the old workings, fork left and ascend
to Coal Clough Wind Farm. The walk continues by turning right
along the Long Causeway, following it up to a brow where the
Pennine Bridleway crosses the road. Turn left and follow the Pennine

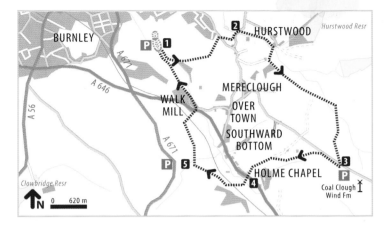

Bridleway as it drops through pastures past Pearsons Farm and then Merrill Head to join a track leading down to the small community of Holme Chapel.

(4) To continue, on reaching the A646 turn right and then immediately left (still on the Pennine Bridleway) onto a broad track leading towards the railway line. Immediately before the railway embankment turn right and, re-joining the Burnley Way, keep on it as it passes under the railway and contours along the side of the valley before climbing first to Scout Farm and then Stone House Fold.

(5) Just beyond this farm with its attractive white cottage, turn right off the main track as the Burnley Way crosses pastures, keeping left of a prominent wooded hill (Spring Gardens on the map but known locally as the Fireman's Helmet). After crossing one wall, turn right in front of the next and follow the track down to pass under the railway and out onto the A646 close to Walk Mill. Turn right and then left into Park Rd. This leads down to Towneley Park.

Points of interest

The fantastical landscape of Sheddon Clough is a result of hushings – a method of mining using the force of dammed water to clear topsoil to reveal the limestone underneath.

Winmarleigh Moss

START The Patten Arms, on the B5272
north of Garstang, PR3 0JU, SD479490

DISTANCE 8 miles (13km)

SUMMARY Easy

MAP OS Explorer 296 Lancaster,
Morecambe & Fleetwood

WHERE TO EAT AND DRINK
The Patten Arms, T01524-791484.
With no other suitable car park
on the route, the pub is the best
place to start; we advise readers to
seek permission, which is always
granted to paying customers

Winmarleigh has the largest area of unclaimed moss land in the county. This
walk takes you across this exceptional landscape.

1. From the car park turn right and walk along the road for 200yds,
then turn left onto a track to the left of a large house. Cross a stile next
to a gate and keep ahead for 700yds. At the first junction turn right
onto the farm road leading to Lathwaite Farm. After passing its first
outbuildings, turn right through the main yard.

2. The route passes the farmhouse on the left and passes through a
metal gate into fields. Keep ahead with a fence on the left. The track
leads to a metal gate. Through this, continue with the hedge on the left
to reach a green utility building in the far corner. Behind this, cross a
stile and then turn left to cross a footbridge. Bearing right, cross the
field to the gated Burns Bridge. Over this, turn left and follow the river
Cocker to Little Crimbles Farm. There is no right of way over the first
footbridge on the left, so continue upstream to cross the second.

3. Turn left and then right to cross the yard of Little Crimbles Farm
and then join the farm road. The farm drive leads past Weasel Wood
on the left to a junction. Turn left and then opposite Great Crimbles
turn right onto Gulf Lane. This area, Cockerham Moss, is impressively
flat. The route passes Birch House Farm, before reaching in another
600yds the large complex that is Moss Edge Farm.

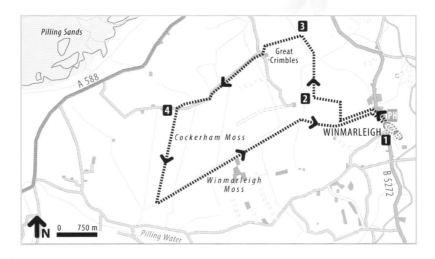

[4]   As you reach Moss Edge Farm, turn left in front of holiday cottages and keep ahead through the yard to reach a track. This crosses fields to reach Poplar Farm on the left and Poplar Grove Farm on the right. After the second farm continue for 100yds to a stile next to a metal gate on the left. As you enter the field, note the ditch on the left. This is Crawley's Dyke, which for the next 2 miles will be your handrail. Keep ahead to a small footbridge. Crossing this, you enter Winmarleigh Moss. After 40mins cross a footbridge in meadowland. Continue with the dyke on the left – now noticeably bigger – as it crosses fields to reach a fenced utility service area. Here, join a track bearing right, which leads back to the point you left it on the outward leg. Retrace your steps back to the pub.

Points of interest

Winmarleigh Moss is home to a number of rare species. Such is the sensitivity of this landscape that visitors are asked to keep to the right of way. Of the total 90ha, 75ha are managed by Lancashire Wildlife Trust.

Great Hill & Belmont

START Crookfield Rd car park and picnic area, BL7 8BG, SD665191

DISTANCE 8½ miles (13.7km)

SUMMARY Strenuous

MAP OS Explorer 287
West Pennine Moors

WHERE TO EAT AND DRINK
The Black Dog,
www.joseph-holt.com,
T01204-811218;
The Belmont Bull,
www.belmontbull.co.uk,
T01204-811370

A superb ridge walk in the West Pennine Moors.

[1] From the car park turn right and walk down to the busy A675 and turn right. After 200yds cross the road to a kissing gate leading out onto the moor. The track is initially stoned and of vehicle width for around 800 yards, where there is a turning circle. It then becomes a wide wet moorland path until it 'disappears' into a reedy area of marsh (around GR 652190). Follow the faint path, leaving the marsh on its right-hand side. Although not definite to start with, it becomes clearer as you progress and swings round to meet a fence just above a wooden stile. Over the stile, descend to cross a small stream and then commence the ascent of Great Hill on a distinct path to the summit.

[2] From the shelter take the Winter Hill sign for a superb moorland yomp along Spitlers Edge, assisted in no small manner by the platform of stone flags leading south towards the masts of Winter Hill. After almost 2 miles (50mins), just below Hordern Pasture, the flagged path peters out, but soon Rivington Rd comes into sight and the now muddier track takes you down to Hordern Stoops.

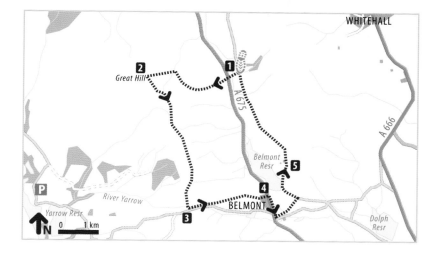

③ When you reach the road, turn left. After 150yds bear left onto a footpath which clings to the edge of the hill. As the path nears the edge of Belmont, follow the direction of a waymark post to a stone stile set in the wall. Keep ahead on the track. At the first houses, turn right onto a footpath that cuts through to Ryecroft Lane. Turn left and walk down to the A675. Turn right.

④ Continue along the A675, and on the far side of the village turn left into Egerton Rd. The lane dips down to the mill complex that once was Belmont Dye Works. Across the bridge on the left look for a footpath obscured by the angle of the road. Take this as it leads upwards to Lower Whittaker. The path goes behind Lower Whittaker farmhouse, then turns right through a small metal gate, then almost immediately left up the farm road. When you reach the lane, turn left. The lane drops down to the southern end of Belmont Reservoir. Bear right to reach Higher Pasture House.

⑤ At the farm turn right between buildings and pass through a large double gate. Continue upwards along a track with a wall on your right. At the junction cross a stile by a large gate, turn left, and along a good track return to Crookfield Rd car park in about 30mins.

START Waddington village
centre, BB7 3HP, SD729438

DISTANCE 8½ miles (13.7km)

SUMMARY Moderate; includes a
steady ascent of just under 1,000ft

MAP OS Explorer OL41
Forest of Bowland

A walk from an attractive village across farmland and moorland to a fine
viewpoint.

1   Walk up through the village, forking right to reach West Bradford
Rd. Turn right. Continue along the lane past the primary school and
then turn left towards Meadow Head. As you approach the house,
cross a stile on the right. Continue upwards to reach another stile in
the right corner of the field. Follow the direction of the Lancashire
Witches Walk – straight ahead. On nearing a large property, bear left
to reach a pair of stiles on each side of a track. Cross these and bear
left around the side and rear of a farmhouse to arrive at a metal gate
at the end of a wall. Follow the direction of the right-hand waymark
pointing diagonally right. After a footbridge and stile, continue
straight across a broad field to a footbridge over a ditch to reach a stile
set in a wall. Keep on the footpath beyond this in the same direction
to come to Moor Lane. Turn left.

2   After 500yds the lane turns left towards Seedals. Here, keep
ahead on the bridleway. Beyond a barn and a pair of wooden gates,
the bridleway follows a wall on the left. Some 500yds beyond the
barn the track turns slightly to the right and then, 300yds further on
before a metal gate, turns right towards a conifer plantation. After
15mins, before a ruined farmhouse, turn left and then soon after right
and you will reach the plantation. Here, turn left on a stony track
and continue the ascent. After 300yds aim for a pile of stones on a
rise. From this fine viewpoint follow the path through redundant
gateposts. Immediately after these take the left fork towards the mast
on Waddington Fell. This takes you to Slaidburn Rd.

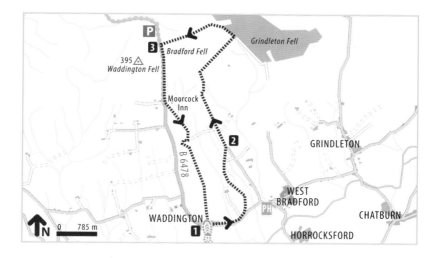

3 Turn left and descend towards Waddington. In ¾ mile, just after the Moorcock Inn, cross a ladder stile on the left. This crosses a large field and then, through a gateway on the far side, follows the edge of a wooded valley. The path soon drops down to the stream and crosses it by a ford. Descend to Cuttock Clough Farm.

Turn right at the lane and follow it over a road bridge. On the left between houses look for a footpath sign, turn left onto a lane and bear left to follow a footpath as it skirts behind a property and then drops to cross a footbridge. Keep left as you climb out of the depression, and keep close to the woods on your right. Before the next farm keep to the right of a covered reservoir and then, after crossing a stile, keep ahead to reach the farm lane. Turn right and after the farm gate left onto a short footpath. After crossing a stone stile, bear right once again with the woods on your right. After 500yds the path bears left to pass through a gate onto a farm track. Keep to the left of the almshouses to reach West Bradford Rd. Turn right for the village.

START Wycoller Country Park, BB8 8SY, SD926395

DISTANCE 8½ miles (13.7km)

SUMMARY Mainly moderate walk with a testing climb to the summit

WHERE TO EAT AND DRINK The Craft Centre, Wycoller, www.wycollercraftcentre.co.uk, T01282-868395; The Old Rock Café, Trawden, T01282-861133

This walk takes you through a lovely hamlet and onto the heights of Boulsworth Hill.

① From the car park take the footpath leading onto the lane to Wycoller. On reaching the hamlet, turn right and follow Wycoller Beck through a lovely vale. After a slab bridge you will arrive at a junction of paths. Yours is the middle way – the Brontë Way.

② This leads up to a farm and then bears left through its yard. After the farm, the route leads gently upwards on a grassy track beside a wall. When the wall turns right, keep ahead. In a short distance you pick up another wall on your right. Ahead, a kissing gate will come into sight, confirming you are on route. A little way after this you reach the junction of the Pendle Way. Turn right.

③ Keep on the Pendle Way for 1½ miles. With Brink End on your left, drop down to an impressive wooden bridge that crosses a deep clough. For the next ½ mile the way follows a rough track. It then dips down to join a utilities service road. After another 600yds, before a farm, turn left onto a reservoir service road now on 'The Boulsworth Circular' path. (If you have no desire to climb to one of Lancashire's highest hills, continue along the track for 800yds to reach a cemented cairn and resume directions at ⑤ .)

④ The way up Boulsworth is steep but the path is clear. The summit is a jumble of gritstone adorned by a trig point. To descend, keep on the path as it crosses the edge of the escarpment. Keep to the left of a wall as you drop below a shelf. At a cemented cairn, turn left.

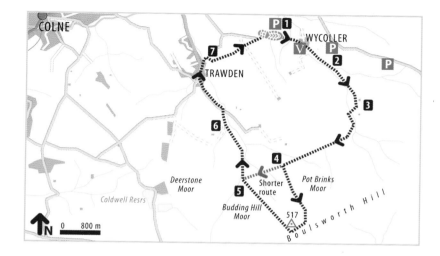

[5] Immediately after the cairn, cross a stone stile next to a gate on the right. Along a grassy path, with a clough on your left, keep ahead crossing two wooden bridges, the second of which takes you across a beck. After a stile the path skirts to the right of a property, bringing you round to a tarmac lane.

[6] Follow this for 800yds to Meadow Bottom Farm. At this point and beyond, any right turn will quickly put you onto the lane leading into Wycoller. However, across from the farm a path leads through a plantation of trees and brings you to a kissing gate. Across the track and a wooden stile, the path leads into Trawden. Walk down the hill. At the parish church, bear right towards the war memorial. When you reach it, turn right into Keighley Rd.

[7] Continue along Keighley Rd and turn right into Stunstead Rd. After Stunstead Farm continue along a narrow lane to Higher Stunstead. Keep ahead in the direction of Wycoller, as indicated on a signpost. At the end of the walled track, enter a field. Here, the main path continues to Wycoller. However, your way back to the car park is left along an unmarked right of way. Head for large farm buildings. On reaching the main farm track, turn left and walk down to the lane. Turn right for the car park, which is 800yds along on the right.

Lancaster

START Aldcliffe Rd, Lancaster, LA1 5BE, SD472608 (roadside parking)

DISTANCE Short route 9 miles (14.5km); long route 11 miles (17.7km)

SUMMARY Length aside, both walks are easy

MAP OS Explorer 296 Lancaster, Morecambe & Fleetwood

WHERE TO EAT AND DRINK The Stork, www.thestorkinn.co.uk, T01524-751234, award-winning country inn

Escape to the country from Lancaster, aided and abetted by the lovely Lancaster Canal.

① Join the towpath of the Lancaster Canal and keep ahead, with the water on your left. After 200yds the canal and road part company. After passing beneath Ashton Road Bridge, the canal enters a deep cutting. Continue on the canalside path.

② For those doing the longer route, keep on the canal until you reach the top lock of the Glasson Arm. Here, turn right to follow the canal through five more locks to reach the basin at Glasson Dock. As you reach the far end of the marina, cross the road and turn right on the Lancashire Coastal Way. Resume directions at ③.

SHORTER ROUTE

As you approach Galgate across the canal, cross a stile in the hedge on the right. The footpath leads to the edge of Forerigg Wood. Bear right and after 150yds turn left and enter the wood over a stile. After 100yds exit the wood by another stile. Keep ahead over a low hill, dropping down to the field corner to the right. Go through a wooden kissing gate and follow the path to a wooden stile, with electricity pylons a short distance ahead. With the hedge on your right, pass below the pylons and go through a gate on your right. Continue with the hedge

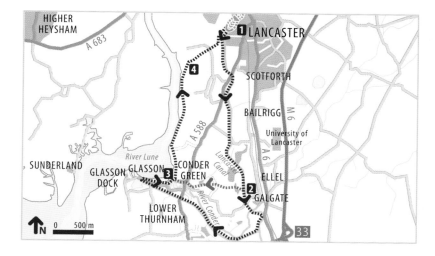

on your left. The track takes you down to Parkside Farm. Keep ahead through the buildings and, after crossing a stone stile, continue with a hedge on your right. Passing Crow Wood on the right, go through a squeeze stile, cross a footbridge and then turn left over a stile. Now with the hedge on your left, pass Webster's Farm to arrive at a lane. Turn right onto the minor road and then aim for the Stork Inn.

(3) Pass the Stork on your right and turn right onto the next lane, leading to a picnic site. Soon after this, you join the Lancashire Coastal Way. Keep on it for 3 miles.

(4) After passing below a double set of pylons that bestride the river, the route passes close to sewage works at Stodday. After 10mins turn right onto a footpath that crosses fields to Aldcliffe. The path is well marked, making use of duckboards immediately over a stile. Keep ahead and then turn left as you enter the adjoining field. With a hedge on your left, continue over a stile. Ignoring the next stile on your left, continue to the next one and then turn left into a green lane. This footpath leads round to Aldcliffe. As you reach the village, turn right into Aldcliffe Hall Lane and then left into Aldcliffe Rd. The road drops down to the canal close to your starting point.

START Car park by St Peter's
Church (please use courtesy
box to make contribution to the
church), Leck, LA6 2JD, SD642765

DISTANCE 9 miles (14.5km) if
ascent to Gragareth is included,
7½ miles (12km) if not

SUMMARY Strenuous

MAP OS Explorer OL2 Yorkshire
Dales, Southern & Western areas

A walk to where Lancashire meets the Yorkshire Dales, with an optional ascent of
Lancashire's highest hill.

① From the car park turn left towards Ireby and walk along the lane
for ¾ mile (15mins). After the lane turns sharply left at Todgill Farm,
turn left onto a farm track that soon starts to climb, first behind Leck
Villa on the left and then Leck Hall. In 30mins the track reaches the
Fell Rd. Turn right.

② This lonely road climbs up to Leck Fell House, which is reached
after another 2 miles (50mins).

③ High on the skyline to the right, look out for the Three Men of
Gragareth – tall stone cairns that seem to brood over the landscape.
If you have time, they are well worth a visit. Keep ahead through
a five-bar gate. Continue along a broad track until in line with the
last outbuilding of the farm. Carefully negotiating a way through or
around the rock fields that cover the lower fellside, make your way up
to the Three Men. This section is particularly steep. On reaching the
cairns, maintain the same direction until you intercept a faint path
that leads to the trig point, which will be reached after 10–15mins.

④ This is the highest point in Lancashire, at 2,058ft or 627m.
(Retrace your steps back to Leck Fell House at ③.) Now begins a
very awkward traverse of moorland to the gill. Facing the farm on

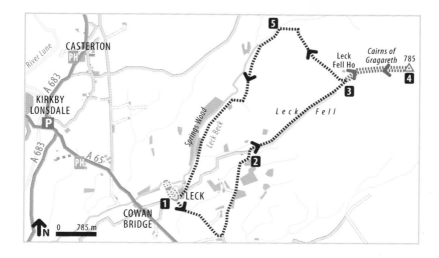

the fell road, turn left at the metal gate. With the wall to your right, you should be able to discern something of a path through bog and marsh, heading towards the valley before you. Bullpot Farm on the fell opposite is a good aiming point. As you come in sight of the gill, bear left on a shelf above it. Follow a fence for 300yds and then turn right through a gate for Ease Gill, which is reached by picking down a faint path. The first thing that will strike you will be the fact that the gill is dry. Near this point, the remarkable geology of Ease Gill Kirk is worth closer inspection. It is an impressive dry waterfall cut into the limestone.

⑤ On reaching the gill, turn left and pick up a path that takes you above a narrow wooded defile and then continues over moorland above the waterfalls of Leck Beck Head. With the stream on your right, follow the path back to the village. About 200yds beyond a ruined farm building, marked Anneside on the OS map, the path dips into a gully. Turn right over a stile and follow a footpath down to Leck Beck. As you near the river, turn left through a lovely wooded vale. The riverside walk is a lovely conclusion to the walk. A track bears left into pastures, leading to Leck. Turn left at the first junction. The lane leads up to a second junction. Keep ahead to St Peter's Primary School. Follow the footpath signs to the right of the main building to reach the church car park.

Downholland

START Carr Lane car park, near
Lydiate, L31 4EU, SD355043

DISTANCE 9½ miles (15.5km)

SUMMARY Flat

MAP OS Explorer 285
Southport & Chorley

WHERE TO EAT AND DRINK
The Ship Inn at Haskayne, http://
canalsideship.co.uk, T01704-840077

A flat and easy walk using the Cheshire Lines Path and the Leeds–Liverpool
Canal.

[1]   From the car park join the Cheshire Lines Path, passing a sign for
Lydiate station on your right. Keep on it for a little under 3 miles until
you reach Moss Lane Bridge, which is clearly signed. It is straight and
level, allowing even the most casual walker to develop a brisk pace.
You may be surprised how quickly you arrive at Moss Lane Bridge.

[2]   Exit from the path, using a slip road on the left in front of the
bridge, and then turn right to cross it. The lane is narrow and cars
have to use passing places to negotiate it. After crossing another
bridge (over a branch of the disused railway), turn left at the first
junction (Riding Lane) and walk to Haskayne. Once in the village,
turn left at the T-junction into School Lane. On reaching the busy
A5147 Southport Rd, cross it with care into Rosemary Lane to reach
the Ship Inn and the Leeds–Liverpool Canal just beyond.

[3]   Turn right onto the canal towpath. You are now walking back
towards Lydiate. The towpath offers easy walking and once more a
good pace can be achieved. To begin with, Southport Rd may seem
intrusive but, after Downholland Cross, road and water part company
for a while. After 2½ miles you will reach Lydiate Hall Bridge (No. 18).
Cross the bridge and turn right onto a wooded footpath that leads to
Southport Rd. Turn right on reaching the road. After 300yds turn left
into Station Rd. Follow the lane as it bends to the left, and then turn
right into Punnell's Lane. Cross Altcar Lane into Carr Lane. The car
park is at the end.

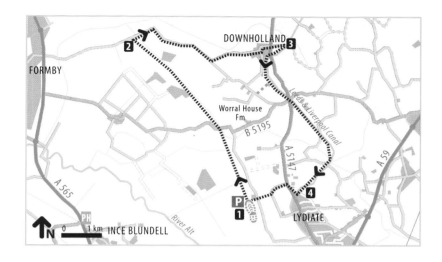

Points of interest

The first part of the walk follows the Cheshire Lines Path. The Cheshire Lines Railway Company that once linked Liverpool to Southport was closed in 1952. Through the work of Sustrans, a national charity that promotes and develops safe routes for cyclists and pedestrians, the disused track has been maintained as a recreational path and cycleway.

As you near Moss Lane Bridge, you are not far from Great Altcar, over to the left, where from 1836 until 2005 the Waterloo Cup was an annual event. The Hunting Act of 2004 made hare coursing illegal, the 2005 meeting being the last before the ban came into force.

This section of the Leeds–Liverpool Canal was the first to be cut in 1770, allowing the Ship Inn to claim it is the oldest inn on the canal. When walking alongside this haven of wildlife, it is difficult to see the canal for what it once was – a vital artery of the industrialized north.

Wolfhole Crag

START Small car park near
Tower Lodge on the Trough of
Bowland Rd, close to Marshaw,
LA2 9BN (nearby), SD604539

DISTANCE 10 miles (16km)

SUMMARY Strenuous; one of the few
walks in this book where a compass
or satnav is required (see ⑤)

MAP OS Explorer OL41
Forest of Bowland

A demanding but rewarding walk to the summit of Wolfhole Crag in the Forest
of Bowland.

① The first part of the walk follows a section of the Wyre Way from
Tower Lodge to Gilberton Farm. From the car park cross the road and
turn onto a track by Tower Lodge. After 300yds turn left at a stone
marker engraved with the Wyre Way logo (WW) and signpost. The
path crosses over rough pastures to reach a ladder stile, which you
cross. Turn right and almost immediately pass through a gate in the
wall ahead. Continue downhill to the wall corner and cross by a stone
stile, also engraved with the Wyre Way logo. Pass through a gate on
your right and follow the track between two outbuildings and over a
bridge. Go diagonally left across a field to reach and cross the infant
Tarnbrook Wyre by a large wooden footbridge. Follow the farm drive
to the boundary wall and turn right onto a broad Landrover track.

② For the next hour follow the Landrover track as it climbs up to
the peat lands of Brown Syke, the source of the Tarnbrook Wyre. (As
you commence your climb, ignore the newer track coming in from
the left.)

③ When you reach a fence, do not cross but turn right. As well as
you are able, follow the fence across the soggy plateau towards the hill
before you. After a junction of wall and fence (note well as you will
return to this spot after climbing to the summit), continue with a wall
on your left. In another 500yds you will arrive at the trig point in the
midst of a scattering of elephant-grey rock.

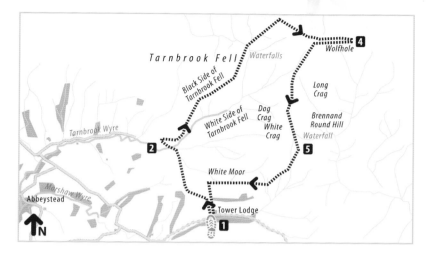

[4] Retrace your steps to the wall/fence junction, pass through a kissing gate and turn left in the direction of Millers House, as indicated by a helpful signpost. The fence on the left becomes a wall as it crosses Brennand Great Hill to drop to Millers House, a traverse of almost 2 miles. If you have built yourself up to see a real house, you will be disappointed. Yep, Millers House is just another pile of stones. Yet rather intriguingly there is an old millstone to be seen, like some ancient carving on Easter Island, indicating this was once a site of industry. Some of the masons seemingly carved their initials on some of the rocks hereabout.

[5] Nearby, a signpost points the way to White Moor. Walk away from the signpost on a 220-degree bearing to follow a barely discernible path, and in a little over 500yds you will reach a wall. Bear right and continue with the wall on your left. Keep with this handrail for the best part of a mile until you reach a gate and ladder stile. Turn left and descend to the Trough Rd.

Abbeystead

START Small car park near
Stoops Bridge, Abbeystead,
LA2 9BQ (nearby), SD563543

SUMMARY Strenuous

MAP OS Explorer OL41
Forest of Bowland

DISTANCE 12 miles (19.3km)

A walk to Bowland's highest point before returning on the Wyre Way.

① From the car park turn left across Stoops Bridge and the infant
River Wyre. On the far side turn right onto a footpath opposite a
large house. Keep on it as it crosses riverside meadows to reach
Rakehouse Brow. Turn left. After 300yds bear right onto the farm
drive of Rakehouse Barn. Follow the track as it bears right in front of
a handsome house (Higher Lee) and then turns left to commence the
climb up to Grizedale Head. This Landrover track provides very easy
walking and navigating. Keep left at a junction of the tracks near the
luncheon hut, and climb more steeply until the ground levels out and
the path along the ridge is reached between Grit Fell to the left and
Ward's Stone to the right.

② Turn right. This path is of a very different character to the
Landrover track. As it crosses peat and heather, it begins to climb
along a shallow, rock-strewn gully to reach the first of two trig points.
Here, there is an impressive gritstone outcrop that presumably gave
the fell its name. Maintaining the same direction of travel from Grit
Fell, i.e. eastwards, look for the second trig point on the horizon. A
boundary stone will be passed after 150yds or so. After reaching the
second trig point, at 1,840ft (561m) one metre higher than the first,
drop down on a more definite path to the corner of a fence. This fence
now provides a handrail to guide you over the next section of the
route. On two stretches the fence becomes a wall. Keep the fence/wall
on your left as you progress along the broad ridge, moving closer to
the next summit, Wolfhole Crag.

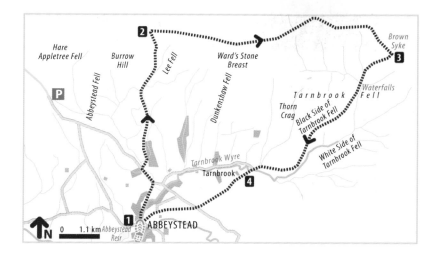

(3) In this way you will intercept a Landrover track that crosses your path, 1½ miles from the second trig point. Turn right. Follow the track as it winds its way down the fellside and, an hour after joining it, you will arrive at the tiny settlement of Tarnbrook.

(4) After entering the hamlet, keep ahead on the main street for 150yds and then turn left onto a footpath that is the Wyre Way. This trail leads most of the way back to the car park. First it crosses the Tarnbrook Wyre, and then climbs the low ridge through a succession of fields to Top of Emmetts. The path is well signed with waymark arrows and decorative stone markers. When Top of Emmetts comes into sight across a large field, turn left and cross a ladder stile followed by a footbridge into the adjoining field. Turn right and, with the hedge on your right, keep ahead to reach the drive of Top of Emmetts. Turn left. Cross the lane and follow the footpath in the direction of Strait Lane. After a marker stone decorated with a hare, bear left in the huge field to follow the side of a plantation to a gate behind a property. The path leads through an enclosure, around a shed and onto Strait Lane. Turn left for Stoops Bridge.

Forthcoming titles in the 100 Walks series

- Yorkshire: West Riding and the Dales
- Derbyshire
- Wiltshire
- Cheshire
- Northumberland
- Surrey
- Staffordshire
- County Durham